ILLUSION WORKS

MORE
OPTICAL
ILLUSIONS

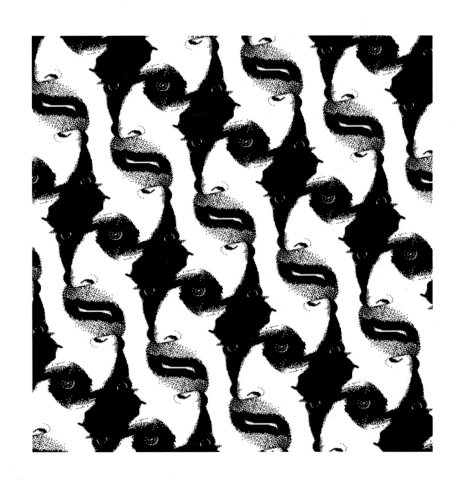

Dedication:
Catherine and Paul Mohr, great friends who have been there for all.

With a special dedication to Martin Gardner, who has inspired so many of us over the years.

Acknowledgements:
I wish to thank the following people who have so generously helped in providing material, or thoughtful criticism: Ted Adelson, Shinko Ando, Jerry Andrus, Stuart Anstis, Chris Banta, Irving Biederman, Jyl Boline, Patrick Cavanagh, Jos De Mey, Sandro Del Prete, Jerry Downs, Thomas Farkas, Martin Gardner, Richard Gregory, Lennart Green, Matheau Haemaker, Donald Hoffman, Akiyoshi Kitaoka, Alice Klarke, Christof Koch, Ken Landry, Bernard Leikind, R B Lotto, Michael Lyons, Andish Martensson, Joan Miller, Catherine Mohr, Paul Mohr, Guido Moretti, Scot Morris, Istvan Orosz, Sinha Pawha, Erwin Purucker, Dale Purves, Vilymur Ramachandran, Oscar Reutersvärd, Tim Rowett, Elizabeth Seckel, Laura Seckel, Mark Setteducatti, Roger Shepard, Shin Shimojo, Dick Termes, Maria Villanueva, Carol Yin. A special thanks to my editor Vanessa Daubney at Carlton Books.

This is a Carlton Book

Text and illustrations©2002 IllusionWorks, L.L.C.
with the exception of the following:
Pages 18, 106 © 2002 Ted Adelson; page 100 © 2002 Shinko Ando; page 54 © 2002 Mitsumasa Anno; pages 62, 89, 98, 123 © 2002 Artists Rights Society; page 32 © 2002 Peter Brookes; pages 66, 69, 140 © 2002 Patrick Cavanagh; pages 15, 57, 72, 108, 116, 127 © 2002 Sandro Del Prete; page 47, 51, 154 © 2002 Jos De Mey; pages 29, 55, 77 © 2002 Jerry Downs; page 86 © 2002 Tomas Farkas; pages 23, 38, 65, 120, 126, 129, 153 © 2002 Shigeo Fukuda; pages 45 © 2002 Robert Greenler; pages 49, 87 © 2002 Matheau Haemaker; pages 25, 99 © 2002 Hans Hamagren; page 70 © 2002 Bush Hollyhead; pages 12, 28, 92, 132, 149 © 2002 Akiyoshi Kitaoka; pages 83, 128 © 2002 Ken Landry; page 9 © 2002 Isia Leviant; page 39 © 2002 Michael Lyons; page 125 © 2002 Joan Miller; pages 19, 76 © 2002 Guido Moretti; pages 36–7 © 2002 Scot Morris; pages 40–1, 146 © 2002 Istvan Orosz; pages 21, 139, 143, © 2002 Dale Purves & R B Lotto; page 14 © 2002 Erwin Purucker; pages 52, 91, 113, 118 © 2002 Oscar Reutersvärd; page 130 © 2002 Roger Shepard; page 13 Pawan Sinha; pages 63, 85, 88 © 2002 Dick Termes.

Design copyright © Carlton Books Limited

3 5 7 9 10 8 6 4 2

A CIP catalogue for this book is available from the British Library.

ISBN 1 84222 487 5

Project Editor: Vanessa Daubney
Project Art Direction: Mark Lloyd
Design: Yolanda de Ferranti
Production: Lisa French

Printed and bound in Dubai

ILLUSIONWORKS
The World's Premier Optical Illusion Art Brand

IllusionWorks, L.L.C. is the World's Premier Optical Illusion Art Brand. Please visit our award-winning website (www.illusionworks.com), which features all sorts of dynamic and interactive illusions, illusory artwork, and in-depth scientific explanations.

For information on the illusion on page 1 please see page 128. Opposite: Modified Hermann Grid: What happens when you move your eyes across this picture? In this modification of the classic Hermann Grid illusion, the intersection points are colored white rather than the yellow of the classic Hermann grid. This leads to the occurrence of a new color effect. Around the spot on which the eye is fixed, the intersections remain white. Away from this point they flash lilac; as the eye scans the picture, the colored areas move, too. When the distance from which the picture is viewed is increased, their number multiplies.

MORE OPTICAL ILLUSIONS

Al Seckel

CARLTON
BOOKS

CONTENTS

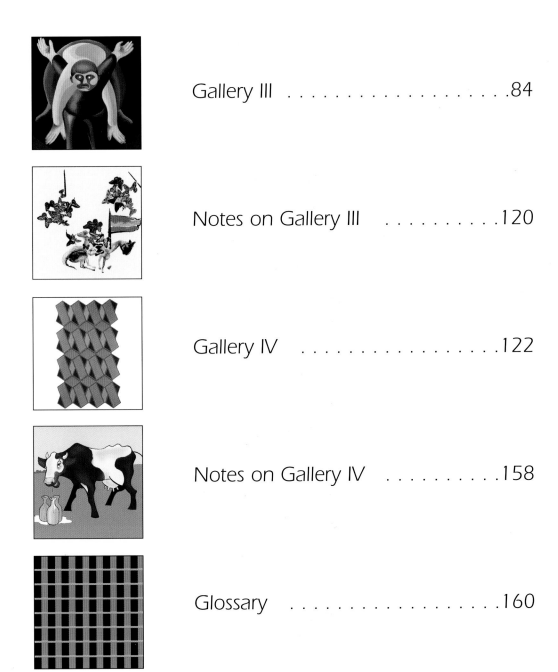

INTRODUCTION

'Perception is the construction of a description'
David Marr

More Optical Illusions is a companion volume to *[The Art of] Optical Illusions*, which was published by Carlton Books in 2000. Many books on illusions reprint the same examples over and over again, but this is not the case here. I have deliberately selected examples that are not familiar, so that the reader has a much greater chance of being surprised.

A number of the illusions and demonstrations come from the results of recent research done in vision and perception laboratories. Other examples come from a variety of artists who have deliberately incorporated an 'obvious' illusion into a drawing, photograph, or sculpture. There are also quite a number of illusions which were specially created for this book.

More Optical Illusions can be appreciated on many levels, and there is enough new and surprising material in here for everyone. Although the book is in a popular format and accessible to all ages, it can serve as a stepping stone to some wonderful projects on perception for students of all ages.

Both *More Optical Illusions* and *[The Art of] Optical Illusions* are laid out in a similar fashion. The illusions are not ordered in any systematic way and are grouped into four different sections. The back of each section contains some notes which give brief scientific explanations of our (and in some cases, my own) best guesses for why these effects are happening and how they are consistent with the processes that mediate normal perception. At the end of the book is a glossary of technical terms which are used in the textual explanations.

It needs to be emphasized, however, that our understanding of vision and perception is very far from complete. We are at the very beginning of our understanding, and many, if not most, of the effects presented in this book are not yet fully understood. Therefore, I sincerely hope that this collection will inspire some serious thought – and practical demonstrations – as to why these effects occur. It is my hope that this may lead to some new insights about the creative intelligence of vision!

Illusions are a nice window into perception, because they can reveal the hidden constraints of the perceptual system in a way that normal perceptual processes do not. You do not see many illusions in the real world because your visual system has evolved so many ways to resolve ambiguity inherent in a retinal image. Visual perception is essentially an ambiguity-solving process. However, mistakes can happen. Sometimes, an illusion occurs when there is not enough information in the image to resolve the ambiguity. For example, important clues which would normally be present in the real world, and would have resolved the ambiguity are missing.

Other illusions take place because an image violates a constraint based on an underlying regularity of our world. In other cases, illusions occur because two or more different constraints are in conflict. This means that your visual system can interpret the scene in more than one way. Even though the image on your retina remains constant, you never see an odd mixture of the two perceptions, although the two interpretations may perceptually flip back and forth.

Many illusions in this book are caused by artists who have intentionally created objects that have 'accidental' alignments, where the true shape of the object perceived is cleverly obscured and controlled from a fixed viewpoint. Nature is normally not so devious, and so your visual system assumes that you perceive objects from a 'generic point of view', unless there is evidence to the contrary.

Part of the fun will involve being tricked, fooled, and misled. This book will definitely do that! It has absolutely nothing to do with how smart you are, how cultured you are, how artistic you are, or how old you are!

Many of the illusions are so powerful you will doubt the written description, while others are so convincing that you will perceive nothing wrong. You will know you are being tricked but you won't know how. Now go have some fun!

Al Seckel
California Institute of Technology, 2002

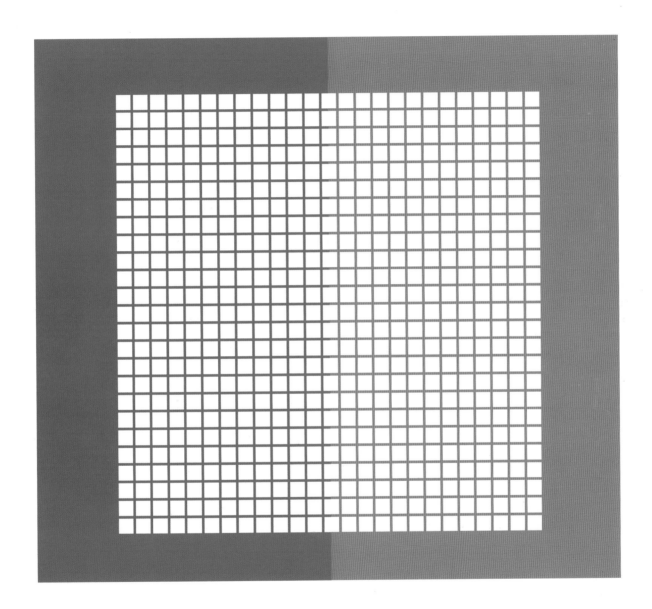

Color Assimilation: Do you perceive a reddish hue within the white squares on the right and a bluish hue within the white squares on the left? See page 158.

GALLERY

I

1 What is this? Can you make sense of this bizarre scene? The photograph has not been altered.

Previous page: **Enigma:** Stare at the circles and you will perceive motion occurring within the rings. They can suddenly change direction too.

2 **A Two Bodied Woman:** To which body does Lady Bird Johnson's head belong in this unaltered photograph?

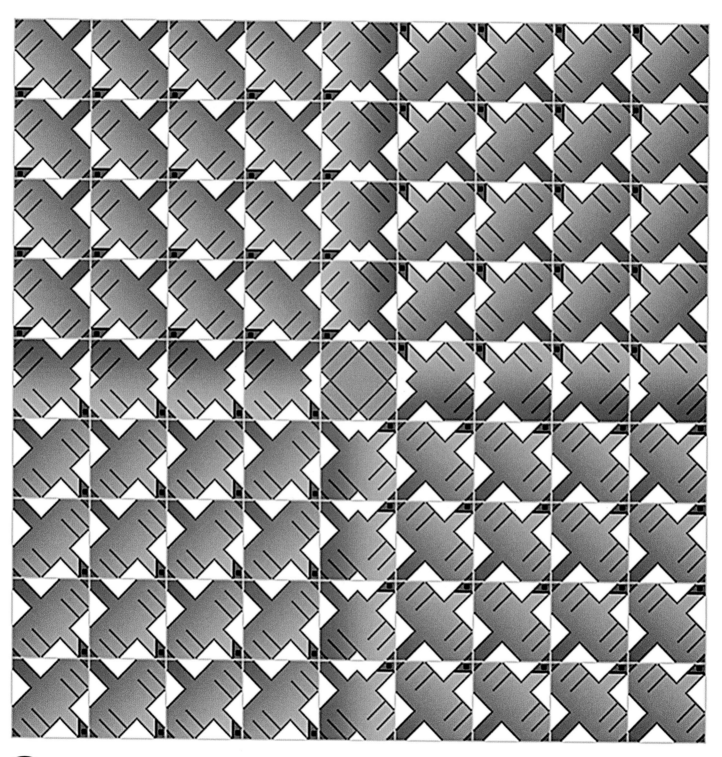

3 **The Café Escher Illusion:** Do the squares appear to bulge in the center? Check them with a straight edge. Japanese artist and vision scientist Akiyoshi Kitaoka created this new illusion, which he calls the Café Escher illusion.

4 **The Presidential Illusion:** How fast can you identify the famous politicians in this photograph? Carefully examine the picture again. You might be in for a surprise!

5 **Tilted Houses:** What happened to these houses?

6 **Between Illusion and Reality:** Look carefully at the two openings. Is this construction physically possible? Try covering the top half of the illustration, examine it, and then separately cover the bottom half. What happens? Swiss artist Sandro Del Prete created this impossible scene, which takes place somewhere between Illusion and Reality.

7 **The Floating Vase:** This vase appears to be floating off the ground, but is it really?

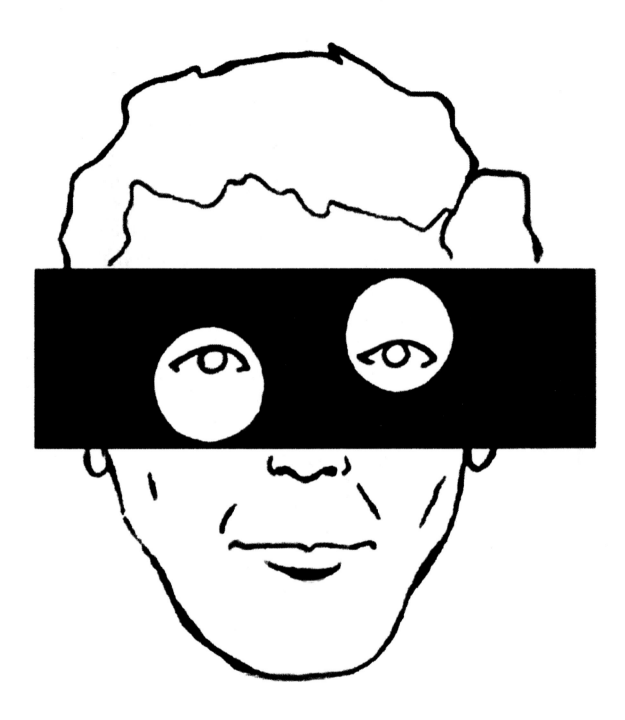

8 **Misaligned Eyes:** Do the eyes appear to be misaligned? Check them with a straight edge.

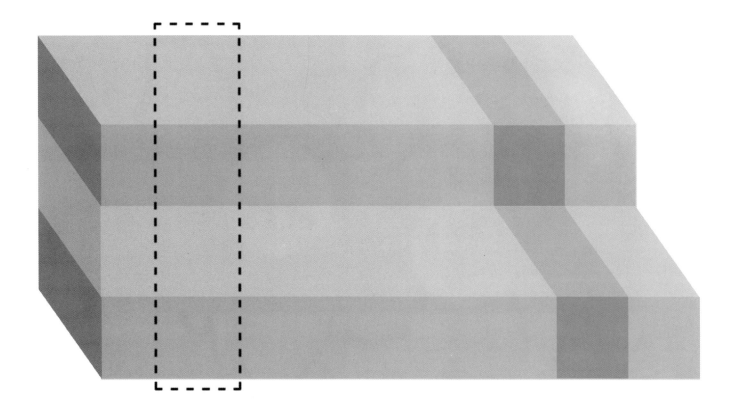

9 **Reflectance Illusion:** There are two illusions in this image by MIT vision scientist Ted Adelson. The stairs look like stacked planks on the left side, but like steps on the right side, which is an impossible construction.

Secondly, there is a reflectance illusion: the dark and light sections on the ends of the left 'planks' are the same color as the gray stripe running down the steps on the right.

⑩ Moretti's Impossible Blocks: Believe it or not, these seemingly different sculptures are three different views of the same sculpture!

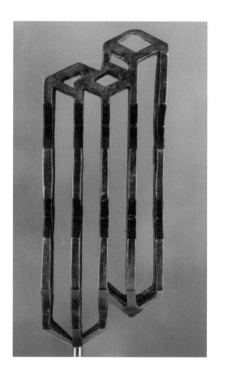

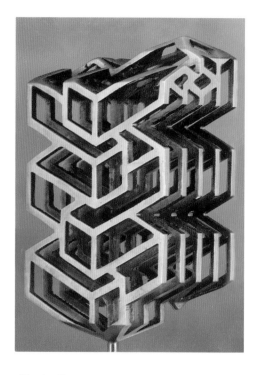

Photo A

From this angle, you will see a set of blocks based on a design by Swedish artist Oscar Reutersvärd – three vertically aligned blocks at the top, which somehow merge into two vertically aligned blocks on the bottom. This construction, of course, is impossible.

Photo B

Turn the sculpture clockwise by 90 degrees and you will see a set of several horizontally aligned impossible blocks, also based on a design by Oscar Reutersvärd.

Photo C

The third view shows the sculpture from an angle midway between the other two. Italian artist Guido Moretti created this remarkable impossible transforming bronze sculpture.

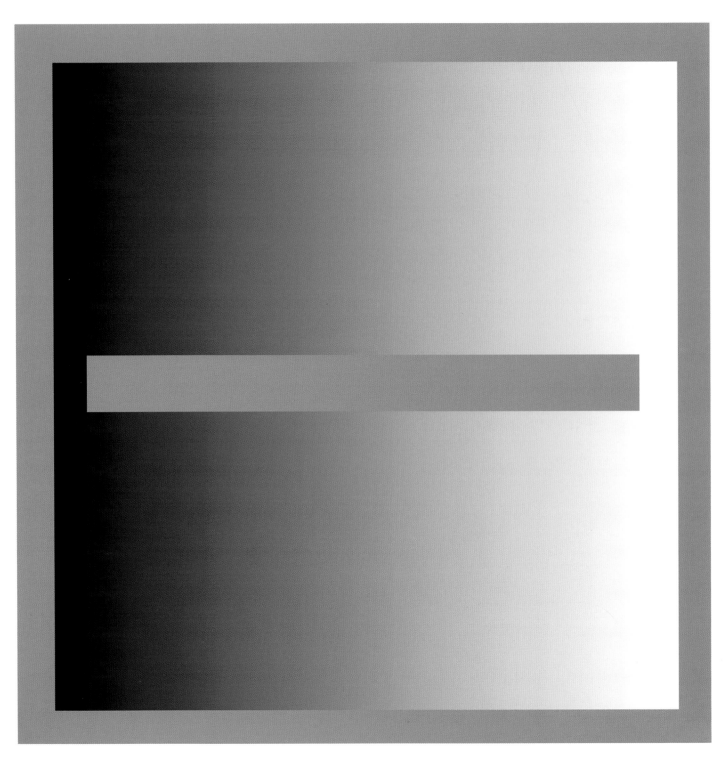

11 **Simultaneous Contrast Illusion:** Is the horizontal bar the same shade of gray throughout? Check by covering everything except the horizontal bar.

Photo A

Without using a measuring device, which angle appears the largest? Which angle appears the smallest? Arrange the angles in order of descending order of angular size if you can.

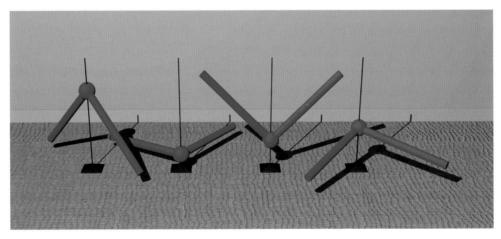

Photo B

Do all the angles appear to be the same size?

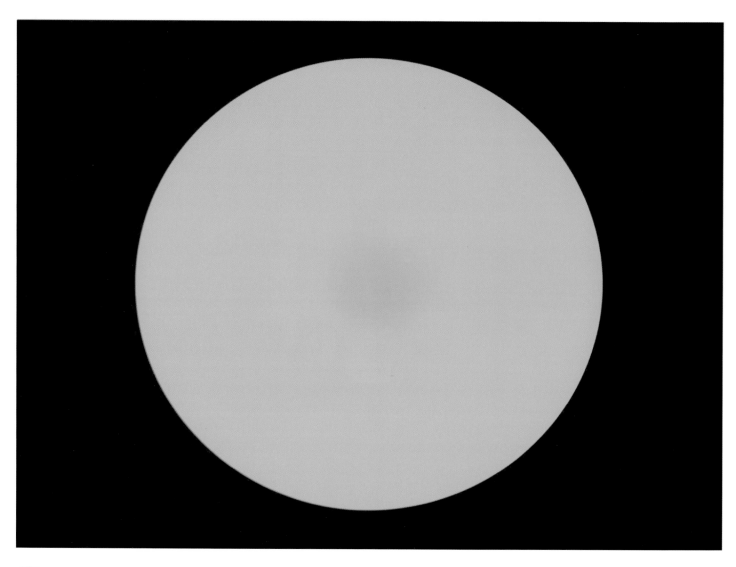

13 **Filling-in Illusion:** Stare at the blue dot in the center of the image, without averting your gaze or attention, and it will gradually fade out. This is a filling-in illusion.

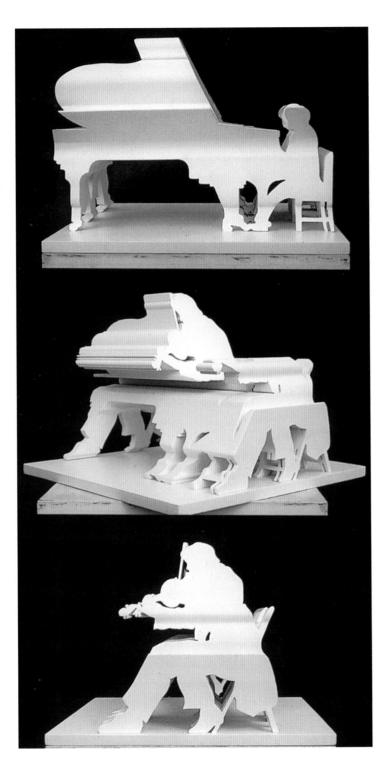

14 **Duet:** A pianist transforms into a violinist in this sculpture by Japanese artist Shigeo Fukuda.

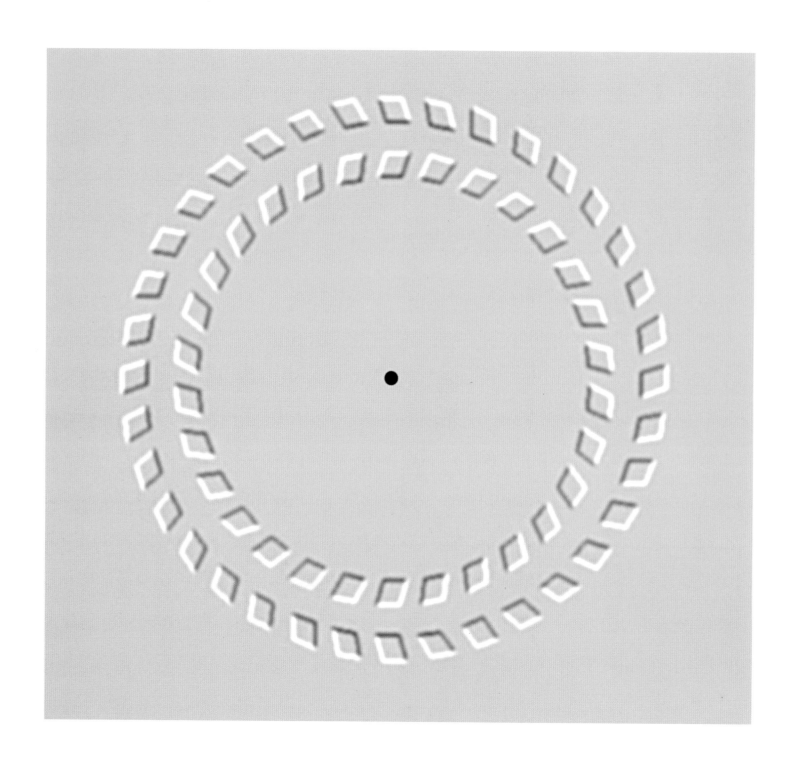

15 **Revolving Circles:** Focus on the dot in the center and move your head (or the book) backwards and forwards. The inner circle should rotate. Try also slowly turning the page.

16 **Leonardo Anamorphosis:** In this painting by Hans Hamngren, the square in the center is blank. When a pyramid-shaped mirror is placed on the square and you look straight down on it (as shown), you see the portrait of Leonard Da Vinci. This Dutch artist created this anamorphic portrait as a homage to Leonardo Da Vinci, who created the first anamorphic image, c. 1500.

17 **The Mirror Paradox:** This is an old paradox about a mirror. When you look in a mirror it reverses the side your hair is parted on. The image in the mirror is left and right reversed, but not top-to-bottom reversed. The image in the mirror reverses left and right, but not top and bottom. Why?

Another way to look at the problem is to lie down on your side and look into the mirror. Your hair will still part on the left side. Your left and right used to be respectively up and down and the up and the down were previously right and left. So, how did the mirror 'figure out' what you were going to do?

English vision scientist Richard Gregory offers an experiment using a match and its box. Hold a match horizontal and parallel to a vertical mirror. What happens? When the head of the match is to the right, its head is also to the right. It is not left-right reversed. However, the writing on the matchbox, when viewed in the mirror, is left-right reversed. So, it appears as if the match and its box behave differently! Why is this?

18 **A Taste Illusion:** Here is a fun taste illusion. Prepare some slices of an apple and a pear. Blindfold your subject and ask him to hold his nose. Place a piece of apple on his tongue. Let him chew it. Can he distinguish apple from pear? Between trials have him rinse his mouth with plain water.

Repeat the experiment. This time he should be blindfolded and not hold his nose. Can he distinguish apple from pear with his nose or with his tongue and mouth? If you hold a slice of pear beneath his nose while he eats an apple, which does he think he's eating?

19 **Kitaoka's Spiral:** This appears to be a spiral, but it is really a series of concentric circles. What happens when you cover half the illustration?

20 **World of Worlds:** A world made of worlds by American artist Jerry Downs.

21 **Falling Bookcase** This bookcase, built by the author appears to be falling. It is based on an original design by Ron Christenton.

22 An Ambulance in an Inside-Out World:

Photo A

This toy ambulance does not look too unusual; however, compare it with the photograph below.

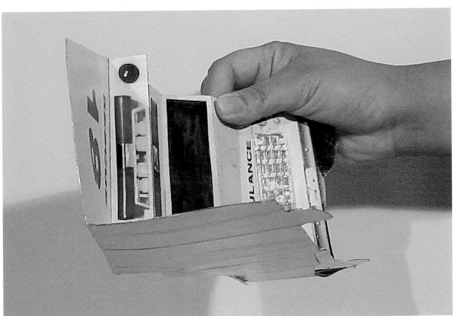

Photo B

The ambulance is really inside out! The inside of the ambulance was painted to look like the outside of the ambulance.

23 **Cat and Mouse Playing Hide and Seek:** Is the cat hiding from the mouse or the mouse hiding from the cat? English artist Peter Brookes created this charming ambiguous figure ground illusion.

24 **Breakfast Before and After:** Can you spot at least two items that are unusual in this breakfast scene? One is easy, while the other is a bit harder.

25 **Magical Chinese Pool:** There is a 'magical pool' inside the Plum Temple located in Zhaoqing, near Guangzhou in China. It was built around 996 AD and has been baffling visitors for over 1000 years!

Photo A

If you stand on the right side of the pool and look to the left, the pool appears to get increasingly shallower.

Photo B

If you stand on the opposite side of the pool, it now appears as if the left end of the pool is deep and gets shallower to the right. This is the opposite of what you saw in the previous image.
How is this possible?

26 **Miracle at the Parthenon:** Is this a miracle? This is an unaltered photograph of one of nature's most beautiful illusions – the rainbow. How did the photographer capture this image of a rainbow on top of the Greek Parthenon? Was it just a matter of luck, or was it something else? The photograph is unaltered.

27 **Jerry Andrus' Crazy Crate:**

Photo A

American magician Jerry Andrus has created a 'Crazy Crate.' How did he manage to connect the straight vertical support beams in such an impossible way? Look at the photograph on the next page to see how he did it.

Photo B
Here the 'Crazy Crate' is seen from another angle, which reveals its true construction.

28 **Shadow of a Motorcycle:** *Japanese artist Shigeo Fukuda arranged forks, spoons and knives to cast a shadow of a motorcycle.*

29 **The Magical Mask of Noh:** The Japanese Noh mask trick dates back to the Kamakura era (1192–1333). The rigid mask was thought to be possessed, because of its 'magical' ability to change expression.

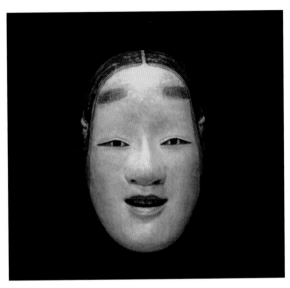

Photo A

Here you see the rigid mask straight on. Compare its facial expression with the two photographs below to see how it changes its expression depending on how the mask is tilted.

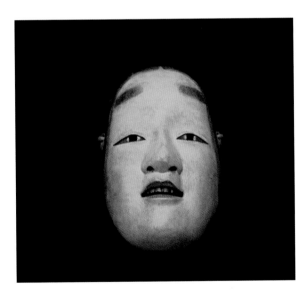

Photo B

Photo C

Photo A

This engraving depicts a scene from Jules Verne's 19th century novel *The Mysterious Island*. Hungarian artist Istvan Orosz hid a portrait of Jules Verne somewhere in this image. It needs, however, a reflective cylinder to see it. Look at the picture on the next page to see the portrait revealed.

Photo B

When a reflective cylinder is placed at a specific point on the image, you will see the portrait of Jules Verne reflected onto the cylinder.

31 Brightness Illusion: Do the black and white squares at the centers of the 'clouds' appear to be different in brightness to their respective counterpart squares?

32 **Cross-Modal Illusion:** Most people would be surprised to learn that one sense can dramatically influence another. For example, it would be surprising to learn that sound can dramatically influence one's visual perception of an event. Here is an interesting description of one such cross-modal illusion.

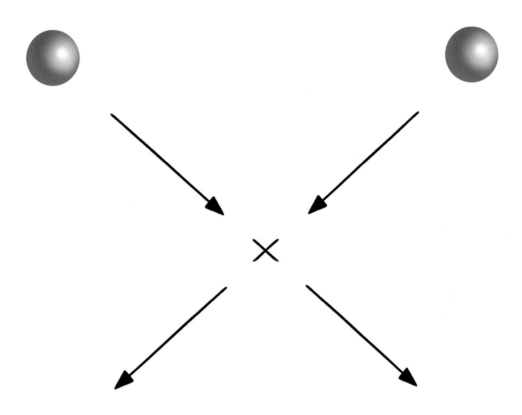

The ball at the top left moves at a constant rate to the bottom right. An identical ball, starting from the top right, moves simultaneously and at the same rate, to the bottom left. They pass through one another at 'X'. This is the motion you perceive unless you make a 'colliding' sound when the balls merge at 'X'. Then you perceive the balls as colliding where the ball that started at the top left ends up at the bottom left and the other ball that started at the top right ends at the bottom right.

Notes on Gallery 1

Enigma (Page 9)

Fixation on the center induces in most, though not all, people a strong perception of motion occurring within the rings. The motion is in opposite directions in different rings and can change direction in any one ring during one viewing. French artist Isia Leviant created this image and titled it 'Enigma', because scientists were mystified about why the effect occurs. Semir Zeki, a neuroscientist at University College, London took PET brain scans of people observing this image, with remarkable results. A specific region of the cortex, close to the area responsible for the perception of motion, was active when subjects had been viewing the display. Therefore, the effect takes place fairly early on in visual processing, after the image is detected, but just before the higher level cortical processing stages where these images are interpreted in terms of previous learning. However, it is still not fully understood what causes the apparent motion of the spots.

1. What's this?

It is a dancer, whose hands are in the shoes and his head is tucked behind one of his arms. Although all the parts of this image are easily identifiable, they are intentionally posed to present an overall configuration that does not conform to your normal experience. Therefore, your perceptual system, when first presented with this scene, has a hard time grouping the familiar parts into a coherent and meaningful interpretation. After looking at this image for a while, you do some perceptual problem solving so that the overall scene takes on a more meaningful and less bizarre interpretation.

2. A Two Bodied Woman

The head is connected to the body on the right. This illusion takes place because the picture was taken from a very special viewpoint in which only one head is visible and appears to be attached to two different bodies. Human vision usually assumes that we are not seeing objects that are accidentally aligned to produce perceptions that are non-veridical. This assumption is called the 'generic view' principle. Some women seem to do better than men in identifying the correct placement of the head because they use fashion clues. There is no reason, however, to believe that the underlying visual/perceptual system is different between males and females.

3. The Café Escher Illusion

It is not completely understood what causes this illusion, but it is known that it takes place very early on in visual processing, when the brain is encoding edges and contours. The Café Escher illusion is categorized among a class of illusions known as twisted cord illusions.

4. The Presidential Illusion

Look closely at this image and you will see that it is not former President Bill Clinton and Vice President Al Gore. Although Clinton is depicted properly in the foreground, the background figure has Clinton's face, but with Al Gore's hair and trademark black suit. This shows how important context can be in forming your perception of a scene, and how seemingly important details can be inadvertently missed. In addition, hairline and width of the head are important to facial recognition. This illusion works best with people who are quite familiar with the Clinton/Gore team. MIT vision scientist Pawha Sinha created the Presidential Illusion.

5. Tilted Houses

No, these houses have not collapsed! They are located on a very steep street in San Francisco. The photographer tilted the camera so that it is level with the street, but not with the true horizon, which is obscured. We tend to align the horizontal and vertical with a reference frame. In this case, the frame is furnished by the rectangular shape of the picture, whose horizontal does not correspond to the true horizon line. A horizon line is a very powerful cue for your perceptual system. Therefore, a misleading horizon line, which is not perpendicular to gravity, can produce all sorts of illusions. The woman augments the illusion by leaning in a way that

appears to be perpendicular to the street. Ordinarily, she would be perpendicular to the true horizon.

6. Between Illusion and Reality

The physical construction of this scene is impossible. Carefully examine the two passages by first covering the bottom half. You will notice that the top half of the passage extends outward. This is perfectly possible. If you then cover the top half of the passage, you will see that the bottom passage extends inward, which is physically incompatible with the protruding top section. The critical transition occurs at about the upper quarter of the panel with the faint people on the left. That quarter is opaque, but the lower portion appears open. This would almost never occur in natural scenes without a definite boundary between the two.

A drawing, however, is only a suggestion of a three-dimensional scene and by itself is not impossible. It is only your mental reconstruction of it as a real physical object that produces a conceptual paradox. Interestingly, your brain does not reject your paradoxical interpretation. This is because your perceptual system is locked into a series of constraints which dictates how it will interpret a two-dimensional image into a three-dimensional mental representation. This demonstrates that the constraints of your visual system are applied to local portions of the image without global error checking.

7. Floating Vase

Shadows can be a very important cue for your visual system in determining relative height and depth. Normally, shadows are 'attached' to objects which are resting on the ground and not to objects floating above the ground. In this scene, the shadow is not attached to the vase, and therefore the image suggests a floating vase. Specially controlled lighting produced this effect. The image was not digitally altered.

8. Misaligned Eyes

The eyes are perfectly aligned. The circles are a frame of reference for each eye, and your tendency is to judge the alignment in terms of the frames of reference. Since the circles are misaligned, the eyes look misaligned. This illusion only works with a simple two-dimensional representation of a face.

9. Reflectance Illusion

If you look at the region within the dashed rectangle, your visual system cannot determine the physical light sources of the stripes. However, if you cover the right side of the figure and view the left side, it appears that the stripes are due to paint. If you cover the left side and view the right, it appears that the stripes are due to illumination (shading) on the steps. If you view both sides, the percept flip-flops according to where you look.

10. Moretti's Impossible Blocks

Moretti's impossible blocks, aside from their seemingly paradoxical structure, provide another sense of surprise to the viewer. They violate one's expectations about shape constancy, which is the tendency of your perceptual system to keep consistent the true shape of objects, even when they are seen at different orientations. Experience dictates your expectation on how an object should transform as you move around it. If you look at photo A, you see a set of vertically aligned transparent blocks. The lines carefully occlude the structure seen in photo B. We normally don't encounter such 'devious' structures in nature, which is why photos A and B are considered 'non-generic' points of view. Moretti's blocks, because of this occlusion, transform in a very radical way – a vertical alignment transforming to a horizontal alignment.

11. Simultaneous Contrast Illusion

The horizontal gray bar is uniform throughout. The color or brightness of the right side of the bar is contrasted with the light background making it look darker, while the reverse happens with

the left side. Current research suggests that this effect is due more to low level contrast mechanisms in vision than to high-level scene interpretation constraints.

12. There's An Angle to This!

In the top photo, although it is hard to believe, all the colored angles are 90° right angles! An image of an angle on the retina is quite ambiguous. We need to know its precise angle in depth. According to Duke University neuroscientists Dale Purvis, R Beau Lotto, and Suragit Nundy, the orientation of the angle exerts a strong bias in the judgment of its extent, depending on the frequency of occurrence of particular angles at that orientation in our experience. Angles at the orientation of the red angle tend to be large and that the green angle tend to be small, so we overestimate the red as large and we underestimate the green.

In the bottom photo, although the angles all appear to be identical, they are in fact, quite dissimilar. So, it is quite possible to make physically different angles appear the same by presenting mutually inconsistent information. Although each of these objects appears to form a right angle, none of them project in this way.

13. Filling-In Illusion

Your visual system only responds to the presence of change in a visual scene. This is because a changing stimulus is more important than a static one. Your eyes are constantly making tiny eye movements, which help to keep the visual scene changing and thus visible. The blue dot gradually fades into the green, because there is no reference for the visual system to gauge the eye's movement, and the steady-state stimulus is gradually ignored.

Almost any stimulus that does not change will eventually be ignored, whether it's a tight shoe, an undersized ring or the beating of your own heart. Pain receptors, however, seem to be relatively free of adaptation, which may account for lingering pain.

In addition, a critical factor in this illusion is the fact that human vision tries to spread color to the nearest luminance defined borders. Since there is no strong luminance between the green and the blue, the green spreads out over the blue.

15. Revolving Circles

Although this illusion is not completely understood, it is most likely due to special properties of low level mechanisms for the processing of visual contours. Italian vision scientists B Pinna and G Grelstaff discovered the Revolving Circles illusion in 1999.

17. The Mirror Paradox

The image in the mirror has neither the right nor the left mixed up with the top and the bottom, but the front and the back have been reversed. The problem is on the axis running through the mirror. If you point north then the mirror reflection of you points south. We think of our image as another person. We cannot image ourselves 'squashed' back to front, so we imagine ourselves turned left and right, as if we had walked around a pane of glass to face the other way. It is in this psychological turnabout that left and right are reversed.

So, what about the matchbox experiment? There is no horizontal reversal. But, of course, one sees the back of the match in the mirror. If you painted one side a different color, the color of the mirror image would be different from the direct view.

18. A Taste Illusion

Your sense of smell is really important in discerning the full flavor of foods. This is because receptors in your nose respond to all sorts of molecules that your taste buds do not. So serving gourmet food to someone who has a bad cold is a waste of time.

19. Kitaoka's Spiral

Kitaoka's spiral is a new variation on the classic Fraser Spiral Illusion. It falls into the general category of twisted cord illusions. If you try to trace out the spiral, you will find that it will induce incorrect finger

33 **Angel Glory:** This natural illusion, which is sometimes seen on foggy mountaintops, has been interpreted as an Angel from Heaven; hence its name Angel Glory. A halo also appears around the shadow of your head.

tracing! Even though you conceptually know that this is really a series of concentric circles, your perceptual system will not correct the error. This shows that even your intellect and your knowledge cannot always overcome the constraints of your perceptual system in how you build up a mental image of the outside world.

The illusions 'breaks' when you cover half of the illustration, because your visual system needs to build a 'global' interpretation of the entire image to draw the inference that it is a spiral.

Kitaoka has made a convincing argument that perceived spirals result whenever lines producing tilt illusions in a coherent direction are converted into concentric circles.

22. An Ambulance in an Inside-Out World
The visual system is biased to see convex interpretations rather than concave ones when presented with a stimulus that is ambiguous in this regard. Lighting is critical in making this illusion work, because shape can be determined from shading. This toy ambulance was inspired by a design developed by American magician Jerry Andrus.

24. Breakfast Before and After
Most people spot that the half-eaten doughnut differs from its reflection in the toaster; yet they miss that the level of the coffee in the cup changes. When you look at a scene, your perceptual system tries to ascribe meaning to it based on past experience. However, your perceptual system does not need all the details of an image to do this – only those parts of the image which contribute to the overall meaning of the image. You disregard the rest.

25. Magical Chinese Pool
The paradox with the perceived depth of the pool is a consequence of the refraction of light as it leaves the water which makes the pool's flat bottom appear curved. The base of the pool is light in color so it

reflects more light than the upper wall surface, and hence we see the brighter image. It works the same way that a one-way mirror does.

The reason that the cement lines in the pool's wall are straight is because these tiles are not under the water, but are actually the reflection of the wall above the water's surface. These cues also make the pool appear deeper at either end. The pool walls are dark, probably the same color as the wall above, but they are obscured by the reflection of the upper wall. Hence you see the reflected upper wall with straight cement lines, as these lines are not influenced by refraction.

26. Miracle at the Parthenon
The photographer knew that there is no definite location for a rainbow, but only his position relative to the sun and the rain. The photographer positioned himself so that the rainbow would end exactly on the temple.

29. The Magical Mask of Noh
The shape of the mask emphasizes certain features, particularly the contours of the mouth. Slight changes in viewpoint will change the relative position of the corners of the mouth to the lips. Our visual system is particularly sensitive to tiny changes in facial features, and thus interprets the mask as having different emotional expressions.

30. The Mysterious Island and the Magically Appearing Portrait of Jules Verne
Artists have used anamorphic images since the time of Leonardo da Vinci. However, it was Hungarian artist Istvan Orosz who took the art form to a whole new level. Formerly, artists would make a straightforward distortion of an image, which would be revealed on an appropriately placed reflective cylinder. The image by itself would just look distorted. Orosz managed to obscure the image in an

overall scene, which could stand on its own without the cylinder.

From a perceptual point of view, this anamorphic print is interesting, because the salient parts of the image are reflected as a meaningful portrait in the cylinder, but the less important and meaningless parts of the landscape do not acquire much significance, and are therefore ignored. This may be due to the fact that recognizing facial expressions and faces are very important for your perceptual system.

31. Brightness Illusion
The black and white checks at the centers of the 'clouds' are identical in brightness to their respective counterpart checks. The 'haze' may be a pictorial cue used to indicate an extreme in luminance. This is a variation on the Kaniza blur brightness illusion.

32. Cross-Modal Illusion
Your perceptual system has evolved a wonderful 'bag of tricks' to resolve the various ambiguities inherent in retinal images. Given an ambiguous stimulus, your visual system will lock onto any reasonable cue that will resolve that ambiguity. In this example, given an ambiguous visual stimulus, a sound can be utilized by your visual system to resolve the ambiguity. However, the sound needs to be made at the point of 'impact'. If the sound comes too early or late, it will not dramatically change your perception.

33. Angel Glory
The Angel Glory, also known as the Specter of the Brocken, is sometimes seen on mountaintops, when you are breaking through the mist with clouds below. The apparition moves as you move and is clearly some magnified projection of yourself. A halo also appears around its head.

GALLERY

II

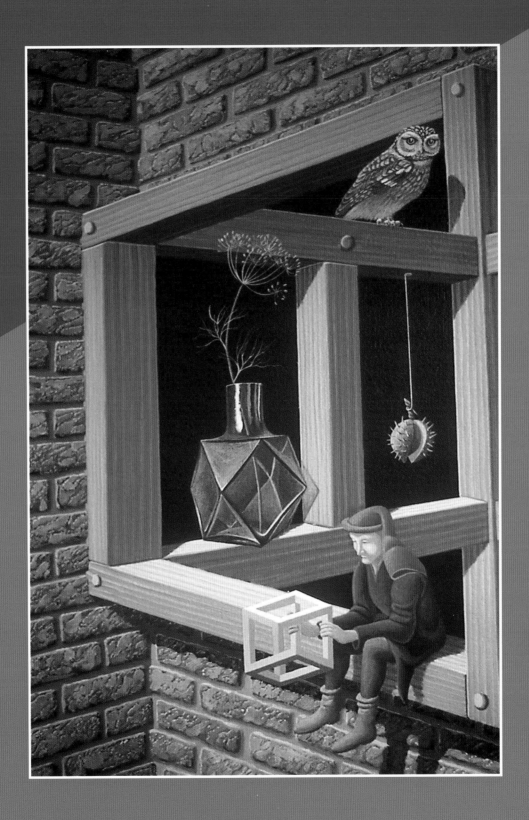

34 **Climbing the Face on the Mountain:** This photograph gives new meaning to the term 'Climbing the face of the mountain'. This rock face is known as 'The Old Man on the Mountain', and is located in New Hampshire, USA.

Previous page: **De Mey's Window:** The little man is contemplating an impossible cube on an impossible windowsill. Belgian artist Jos De Mey created this lovely setting.

35 **Haemaker's Cube:**
Photo A

It is difficult to determine the true shape of this 'impossible cube' sculpture by Belgian artist Matheau Haemaker when seen from only this angle. Compare this view with the adjoining photograph of the same sculpture taken from another angle.

Photo B
What appeared to be straight lines were really curved lines.

36 **An Illusion for the Birds:** On an island off the coast of Maine, in the USA, a puffin, left, stands among three decoy puffins placed there by the National Audubon Society, a conservation group. Because of over hunting, puffins vanished in the 1800s from their island homes. Now people are trying to lure them back. It appears that the decoys are working. So, birds can be fooled too!

37 **An Aqueduct for the Future:** There is something strange about the aqueduct depicted in this scene by Flemish artist Jos De Mey. What is it?

38 **A Different Type of Perspective** Swiss artist Oscar Reutersvärd confounds us with another one of his impossible illustrations.

39 **Stretched Heads:** The heads on these three figures are strangely distorted. Can you find the angle at which to look at them so that they appear normal?

40 **Anno's Village:** Japanese illustrator Mitsumasa Anno is famous for creating unique worlds. This village can be seen upside down as well as right-side up.

41 **Looking for a Sign of the Moon:** Examine this image. What do you see? Remember that first impressions are not always correct.

42 Off the Wall: This woman appears to be leaning off the edge without falling. There are no hidden devices or ropes to hold her up.

43 **The Festival of Bacchus:**
Look at the three scenes
carefully to see how the
two people transform into
the face of Bacchus.

44 **The Glass Rim Illusion:** Visually estimate, but do not mathematically calculate, the circumference of the glass rim. Would you say that your estimate is less than, equal to, or more than the height of the glass? If you had a piece of string equal in length to the circumference of the rim and put one end at the top of the glass with the rest of it hanging down by the side, how far would it extend?

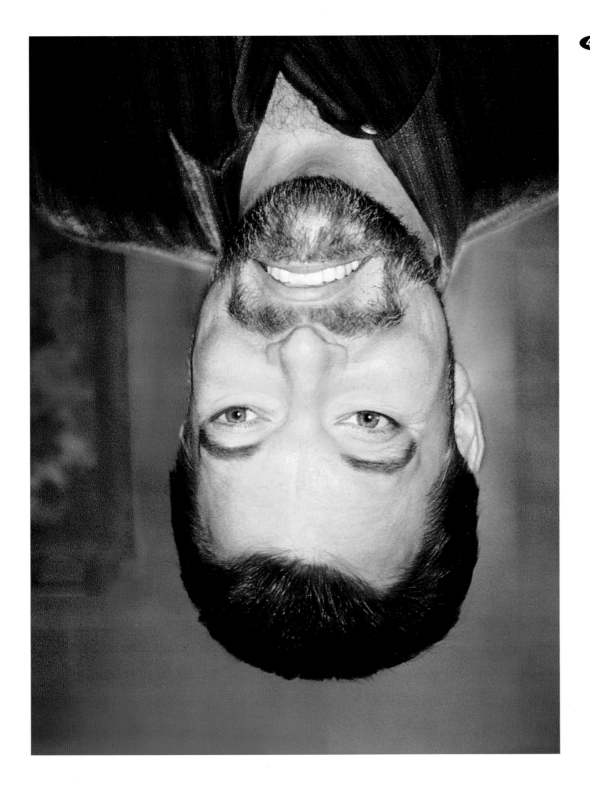

46 **Loch Ness Monster:** *Illusions can often be formed by context and expectation. This floating log would never be mistaken for anything but a floating log, except to tourists on Loch Ness. A tourist photographed this log thinking he had captured on film the elusive and famous monster.*

47 **Impossible Terrace:** Are you looking at this structure from above or below? Notice how the ladder also twists in an impossible way. This scene is based on Swiss artist Sandro Del Prete's impossible drawing, 'The Folded Chess Set'.

48 **Waves:** Move the picture back and forth and you will see the waves move. American op artist Bridget Riley, who created this image, loved to experiment with images which created the illusion of apparent movement.

49 **Eye am a Mouth:** The eyes become the mouths in this charming ambiguous drawing by American artist Dick Termes.

Can you make this policeman look surprised?

X91086

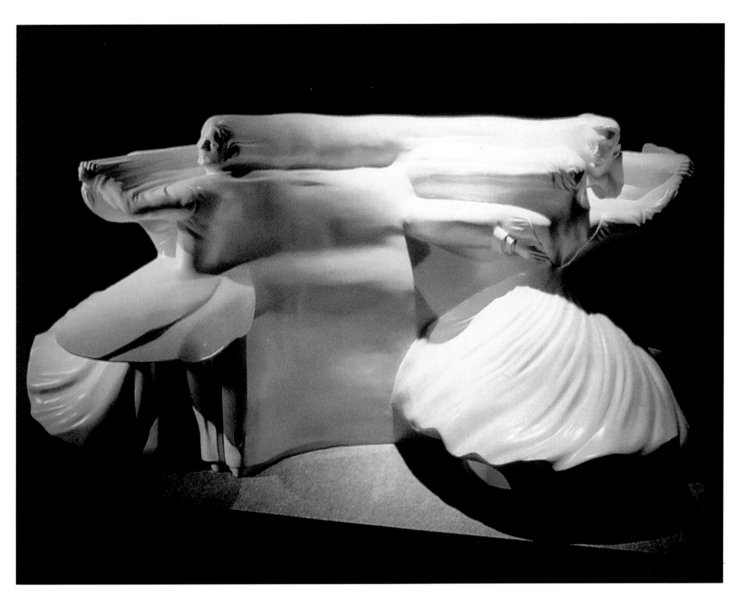

51 **An Illusion of Motion:** Japanese artist Shigeo Fukuda depicts the illusion of motion in this beautiful sculpture of a dancer.

52 Negative Mountains:

Photo A

Compare the two photographs of the same mountain scene. One of these images is the normal photograph, while the other is its negative. Which is which? What clues provide the answer?

Photo B

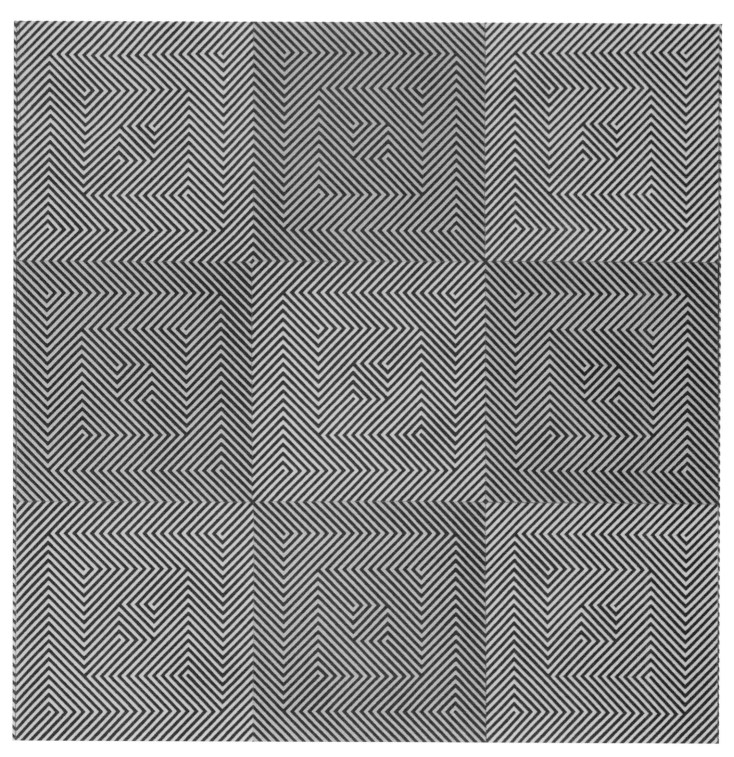

53 **Square of Three:** Move this image and it will vibrate and shimmer.

54 **Antisolar rays:** Do the rays of the sun appear to converge at a point just behind the clouds?

55 **Half Faces:** Which face appears happier?

56 **A Strange Coincidence:**
British illustrator Bush
Hollyhead captured this
bizarre scene at the Fox
tavern.

57 **Crazy Street:** Up and down are perceptually reversed when walking on a crazy street. When you are physically walking downhill, you swear that you are walking uphill and vice versa.

58 Window Gazing: This window is great for looking in two different directions simultaneously! Swiss artist Sandro Del Prete wanted to depict how the world would look if one could look in two different directions at once.

59 **Moon Illusion:** The Moon Illusion is one of nature's most famous illusions. The full moon, just over the horizon, appears to be roughly one and half times the size that it appears to be when it is high over the horizon. The actual angular size of the moon does not change between the two locations.

This doctored picture represents the relative sizes of the horizon and zenith moon, as it would appear to an observer. Interestingly, it is an effect that can't be captured on film. It has to be seen naturally to be appreciated.

60 **Change Blindness:** Compare this photograph with the photograph on the next page, but NOT simultaneously. Flip back and forth between the images to see if you can find the difference.

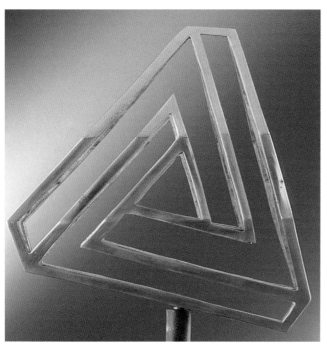

Photo A

61 **Impossible Triangle to Necker Cube:** These three photographs depict the same bronze sculpture as seen from three distinct views. From one view it looks like an impossible triangle a and from another angle it looks like a wire cube. Look at photograph C to see the intermediary form. Italian artist Guido Moretti created this sculpture.

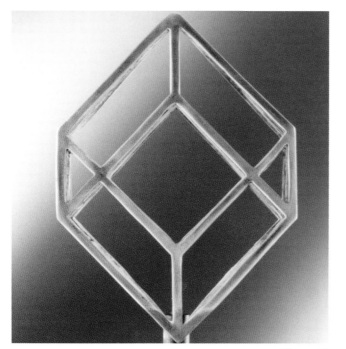

Photo B

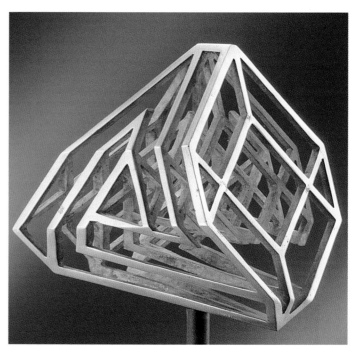

Photo C

62 **A Cat Hidden in its Own Shadow:** Is the black cat walking on a gray pavement or on the grass? Which is the shadow and which is the cat? Rotate the image by ninety degrees in a clockwise direction to be sure.

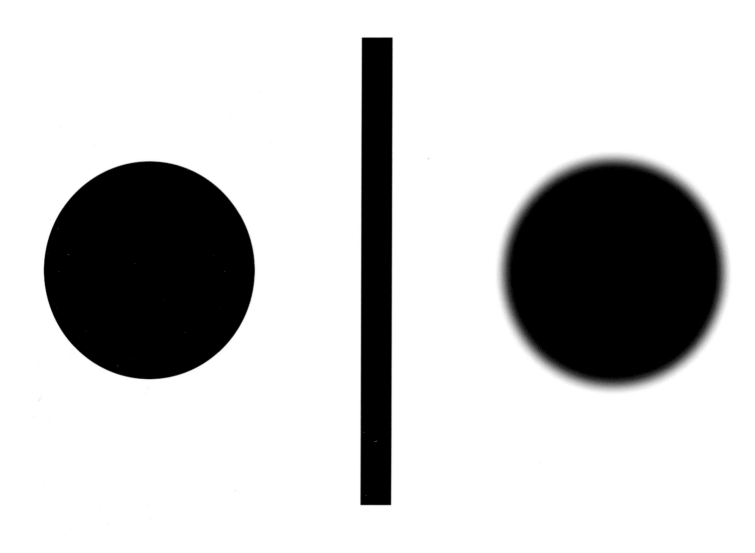

63 **Kanizsa Blur:** Does the right disk appear as dark as the left disk?

64 **School of Fish:** Stare at the fish in this illustration and they will face left and then suddenly change direction and face right.

65 **Topsy Turvy Coin:** This coin from the mid 1500s is the first known example of a topsy-turvy illusion. In one orientation it is the Pope and when you turn it upside down it becomes the Devil. These propaganda coins were popular during the Reformation.

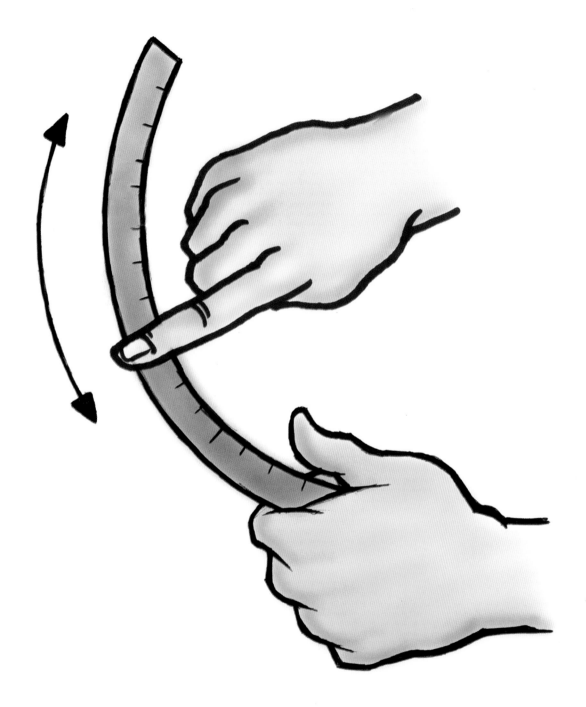

66 **A Tactile Illusion:** Take a bent metal rod and continuously stroke it for about a minute or more. Quickly shut your eyes and then stroke an identical straight rod. The straight rod will now feel bent.

Notes on Gallery II

35. Haemaker's Cube
This is another object which violates shape constancy. You have an expectation that this sculpture will transform in a normal way consistent with past experience. This cube is made out of curved sections, which appear straight when viewed from a single point of view. See also the explanation for illusion number 10.

37. An Aqueduct for the Future
The top part of the aqueduct is perpendicular to the bottom part, which would be physically impossible to connect in this fashion.

39. Stretched Heads
Hold the book at waist level and tilt the top part of the page away from you and look along the bottom edge towards the top of the page, so that the image is almost inverted, as seen in the inset. English artist E. Purcell created this anamorphic cartoon in 1822.

41. Looking for a Sign on the Moon
The round disk is not the moon, but the back of a railway sign. Context, not actual features, will mislead most people in this image. Jerry Downs created this contextual illusion.

42. Off the Wall
This is another example of an illusion caused by a misleading horizon line. The woman is really perpendicular to the true horizon, but the true horizon is obscured from the viewer. The room is actually tilted by approximately 26 degrees. The misleading horizon line of the room causes the viewer's internal frame of reference to change and thereby produces the illusion that the woman is leaning and not the room. This orientation illusion can be found in many tourist attractions around the United States.

44. The Glass Rim Illusion
Most people estimate that the circumference around the glass rim is less than the vertical length of the glass. If you measured the rim with a string, and then held it beside the glass it would extend from the top of the glass all the way down to the tabletop, which is consistent with elementary geometry. Try this experiment at home with the cardboard from a toilet paper roll. Which is greater: the circumference of this cylinder, or its height when stood on its end? Cut the toilet paper roll perpendicularly and you'll find the circumference is the longer edge of the resulting rectangle.

In both cases, the illusion is due in part because the lip of the glass is foreshortened and the length of the glass is not foreshortened at all.

45. The Inverted-Face Illusion
We have special areas of our brain devoted to processing faces, including their identity, emotion, gender, and direction of eye gaze. Because our experience with faces is almost exclusively with upright faces, these brain areas have become specialized for processing only upright faces. In particular, we are inefficient at interpreting the emotions of inverted faces. Because the face is initially upside down (only the eyes and the mouth are inverted), this facial area is inactive. When you turn the face right side up, you see the extreme nature of the expression. It has been demonstrated that some species of monkeys, which hang from trees, and routinely see upside down faces, do not have this face inversion effect.

English vision scientist Peter Thompson using a picture of the former English Prime Minister Margaret Thatcher originally created this illusion. Here we carry out the illusion on actor Jonathan Frakes.

48. Waves
The apparent motion here may be produced by contour – activated cells with receptive fields centered at different positions in the visual field – just as occurs with real motion. The undulation may be a consequence of an upper portion of a contour stimulating cells which were previously excited by a lower portion and vice versa.

51. An Illusion of Motion
Japanese artist Shigeo Fukuda used a cultural device to describe 'the illusion of motion'. Most likely you understood what he was trying to depict, because you are used to the popular convention of suggesting movement in static figures by 'motion blurs'. If you look, for example, at static images of automobile advertisements (where the car is ostensibly in motion), you will notice that digital artists have blurred the wheels. This is an artificial convention that we unconsciously accept, but don't actually see in nature. In fact, viewing a photograph of a moving object without a motion blur now looks strange to us. This is an example of a visual cue that has been artificially introduced into our perceptual organization of the world.

52. Negative Mountains
Many people incorrectly believe that the mountain with the snow is the real image. In fact, it is the negative. What people believe is 'snow' is actually the shadows of the mountain. Photo B is the positive

53. Square of Three
This illusion is similar in effect to number 48 'Waves'.

Many Op artists explored such effects in their works, including the famous painter Bridget Riley. American artist Reginald Neal created this work, which he entitled 'Square of Three'.

54. Antisolar Rays
The sun's rays are actually parallel, but due to perspective effects, they seem to converge.

55. Half faces
Many people see the right face as happier, even though the faces are mirror-images. The facial expression of the left face has a greater impact on our interpretation of a person's emotion. There is some controversy on whether this asymmetry stems from the fact that the right hemisphere of the brain is more dominant in the processing of facial expressions.

57. Crazy Street
This is another illusion which is caused by a misleading horizon line. The true horizon is kept out of sight from the observer. Normally, the true horizon is perpendicular to gravity, but in this case, vestibular information from your inner ear, which provides us with information about the true direction of gravity, is at odds with your perception of your view of the 'misleading' horizon. This causes an illusion where up and down are somewhat reversed. This is another example of a cross-modal interaction, where one sense influences another.

59. Moon Illusion
The moon illusion has created quite a controversy about what gives rise to the effect, and there are many explanations for why the illusion occurs. The only agreement seems to be that it is not an atmospheric effect.

Part of the complication stems from the fact that there are many visual cues which the brain relies on when assessing size and distance relationships. These cues work fairly well for objects which are relatively nearby, but they tend to break down for objects that are extremely distant, such as the moon, planets, stars, and so forth. Also, the moon illusion is difficult to recreate in an unnatural setting. It does not work at all in a planetarium. Double exposures of the moon taken at both its horizon and zenith positions also destroy the illusion. Separate pictures of both positions also fail to capture the illusion. Therefore, it appears only to work in a natural environment. This is in contrast to many size–distance illusions, which can be reproduced photographically or by illustration.

Normally, when objects recede into the distance against a perspective background, not only does their visual angle get smaller, but they also approach a visual horizon. The moon, because of its enormous distance from us, does not change its visual angle much (only about 2 per cent) as it traverses across the heavens. However, your perception of its size does change. This is because your brain is interpreting the image on your retina based on visual cues that it uses for assessing the size and distance of objects in proximity, i.e, between the visual horizon and you.

Also, your visual system tends to be quite good at assessing the size and distance of objects which are resting on the ground, but your visual system has a much harder time assessing the distance of objects that are not 'attached' (floating) with respect to the ground. It is even more difficult for your visual system to assess the proper size and distance of objects if a perspective background has been removed, as in the case with the moon in its zenith position. In fact, there are many other visual cues that are used by the visual system in assessing size and distance relationships, such as ground texture or terrain, angular distance, relative alignment of the object to the true horizon (the moon has no such alignment, being a disk), lens accommodation, surrounding objects, and so forth. These visual cues more or less act in unison, but if they are conflicting with each other, you can get a size distance illusion.

When the moon is on a far horizon, all the intervening details suggests that it is very far away. When the moon is at its zenith position, there are also far less intervening cues available. It is the combination of these factors where your brain is interpreting the same object in a variety of conditions, that gives rise to the moon illusion.

60. Change Blindness
The shadow of the water heater has been digitally removed in the second photograph. This change is difficult to detect because you cannot maintain a detailed memory of either photograph, and must compare items in the two photos individually, or in small groups. In other words, one has to do a systematic visual search pattern to find the change, otherwise you are 'blind' to it.

62. A Cat Hidden in its Own Shadow
The intersection between the gray wall or pavement and the grass is ambiguous, so it is difficult to tell whether the gray area is a vertical wall or pavement. Hence, it is confusing to determine whether the cat's shadow is on the grass or on the wall. However, there are a variety of small cues, such as two ears on the cat, one ear on the shadow, that do give away the fact that the cat is walking on the gray pavement. Jerry Downs captured this interesting ambiguous scene.

63. Kanizsa Blur
The right disk does not appear as dark as the left disk, even though they are the same color. The blur of the edges looks brighter (grayer) than the sharp edge, and that edge information is carried across the surface of the disk. Italian vision scientist Gaetano Kanizsa discovered this illusion.

66. A Tactile Illusion
This is an example of a muscular aftereffect. UCSD vision scientist Stuart Anstis discovered this fun tactile illusion.

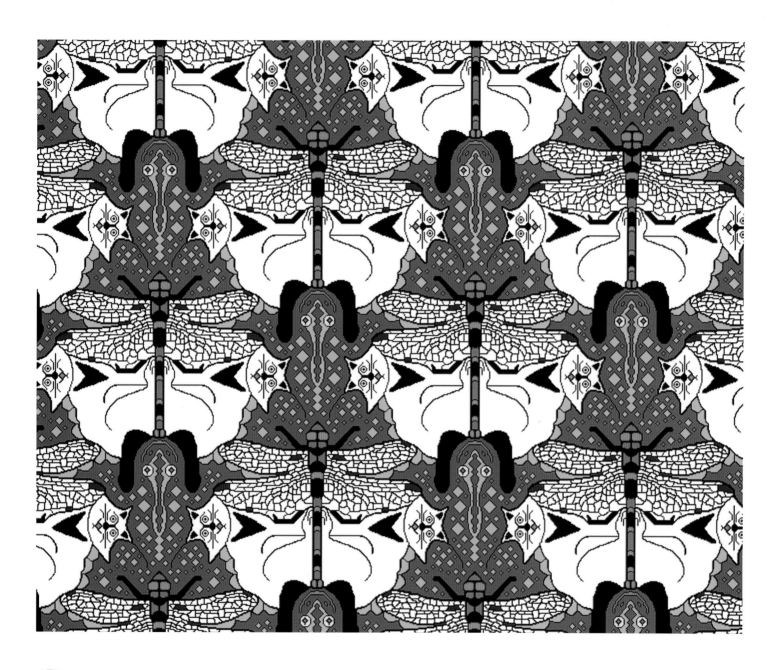

67 **Tessellating Cat, Frog, Dragonfly:** Can you find the dragonfly, cat, and frog in this tessellating pattern by American artist Ken Landry?

GALLERY

III

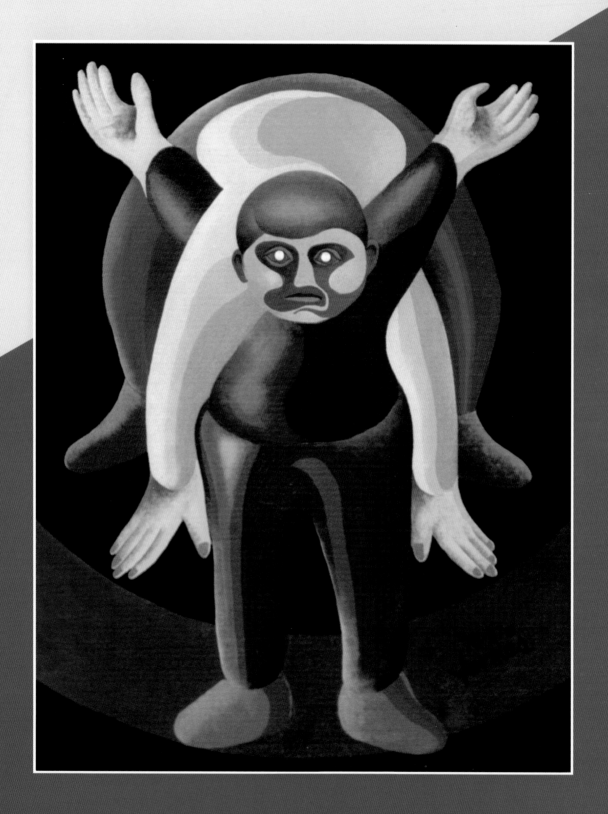

68 **Sidewinder:** Imagine climbing this set of stairs by Hungarian artist Tomas Farkas. If you start out vertically and walk around, you will end up at the starting point in a horizontal position. Oxford mathematician Roger Penrose came up with a similar design some years earlier.

Previous page: **Two Bodies with One Head:** Which body belongs to the head in this fanciful creation by American artist Dick Termes?

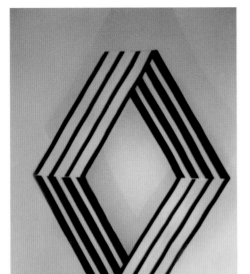

Photo A

This is a three-dimensional sculpture of an impossible rectangle by Belgian artist Matheau Haemaker.

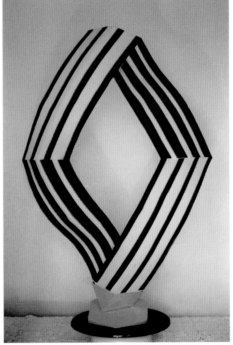

Photo B

When the sculpture is slightly rotated, one can see that it did not transform the way one would have expected. What appeared to be straight edges are actually curved.

Photo C

Here the sculpture is turned at an angle where you can really see its true shape.

70 Numbers Setting 3 Free:
Here the numbers 0–9 are setting the number 3 free. Can you find the numbers 0–9? American artist Dick Termes created this charming illustration.

71 **Strange Scene on an Island Postcard:** Spanish surrealist Salvador Dalí created this ambiguous scene after being inspired by a scene on a postcard. Try turning the image by 90 degrees clockwise to see the face.

72 Miniature Theater: The two girls are life-sized, but they look tiny when seen through the aperture in this miniature theater.

73 **Reutersvärd Triangle with a Twist:** Can you spot the impossibility in this drawing by Swedish artist Oscar Reutersvärd?

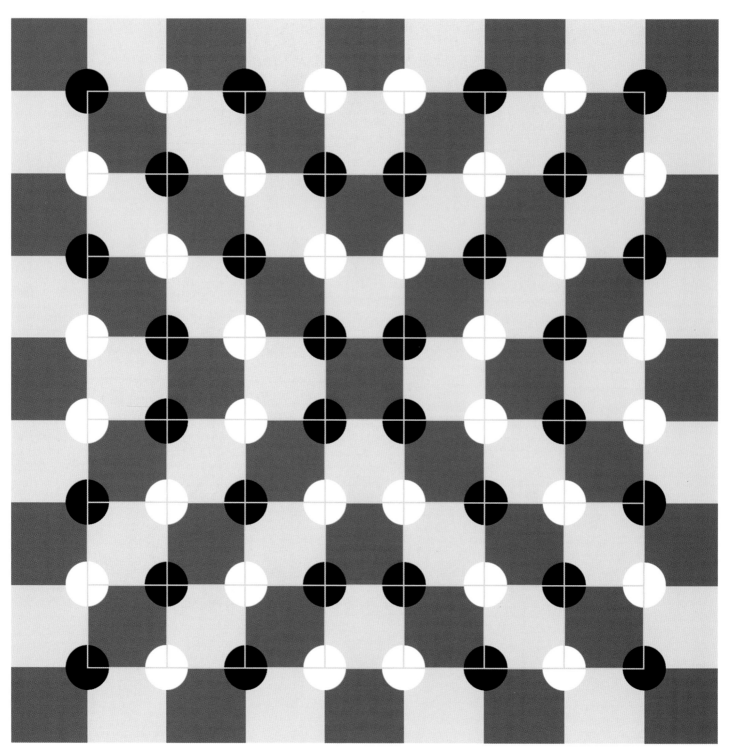

74 **Bulging Lines:** Do the lines appear to be straight or distorted? Check them with a straightedge.

75 **Cosmic Wheels:** The 'Cosmic Wheels' unleash the powers of the universe in this illustration by Swiss artist Sandro Del Prete.

76 **Oops:** Oops. . .

77 **Hidden Illusion:** There is an image hidden within the vertical lines. Try moving the image from side to side to see it.

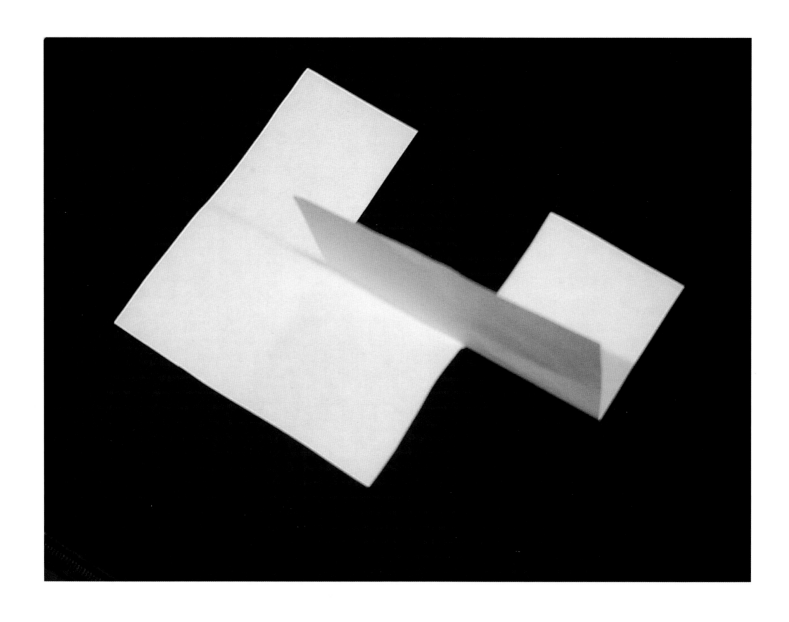

78 **Impossible Fold:** How was this paper folded to create this effect? It appears to be impossible. A rectangular sheet of paper was cut in only two places. No gluing or taping was allowed. See if you can figure it out.

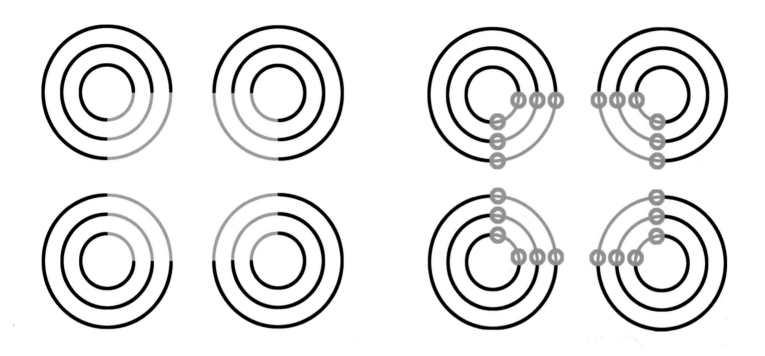

79 **Neon Color Spreading:** Do the insides of any of the two squares appear to have a slightly bluish tint?

80 **Carte Blanche:** Are the horse and rider on the tree or behind the tree in this painting by René Magritte?

81 **Dali Anamorphosis:** This painting has a blank circle in the middle of it. Only when a cone-shaped mirror is placed on the circle and you look into the point of the cone (as shown) you see a portrait of Dali. Dutch artist Hans Hamngren created this anamorphic homage.

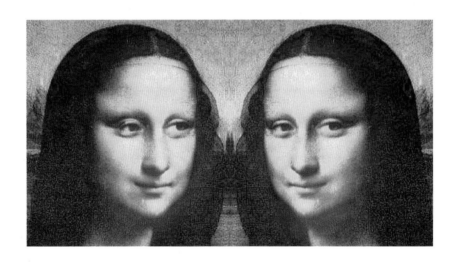

82 **Perceived Gaze Illusion:** Which Mona Lisa is looking at you? Does the direction of her gaze appear to be different?

83 Tiger Photomozaic: This tiger photomoziac was created entirely out of animal pictures.

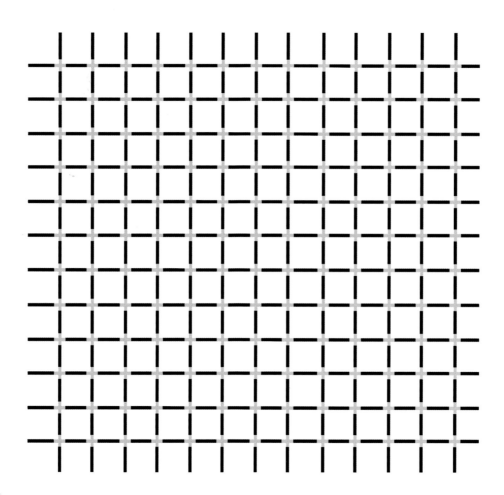

84 **Neon Color Spreading 2:** Do you see bluish disks at the intersections?

85 **Mirror Symmetry of Faces:** One of these faces of Hillary Clinton is distorted. How is it distorted? Taken by itself, does the distorted face look peculiar? This is not meant to be a political satire.

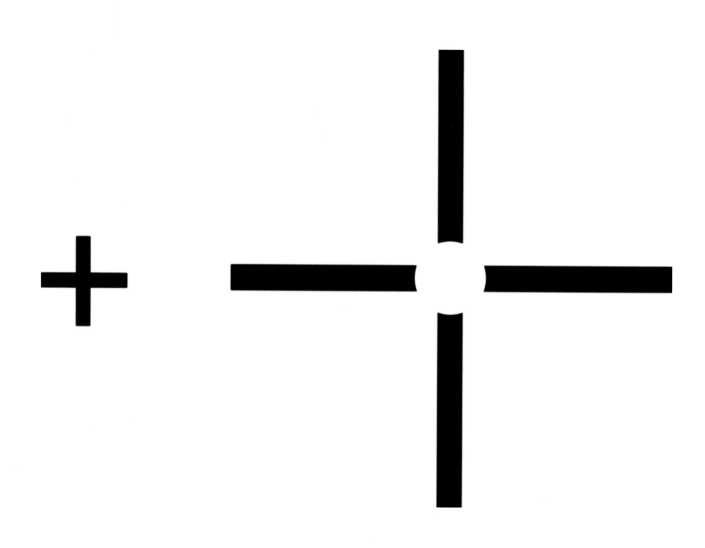

86 **Blind Spot Illusion:** This is a blind spot illusion. Find your blind spot by first closing your right eye. Simultaneously looking at the small black cross with your left eye while moving the image nearer or closer until the white disk disappears. What does the central portion of the completed cross look like? Many people will see the vertical bar in front of the horizontal bar.

87 **Day's Sine Illusion:** Are all the vertical line segments the same length?

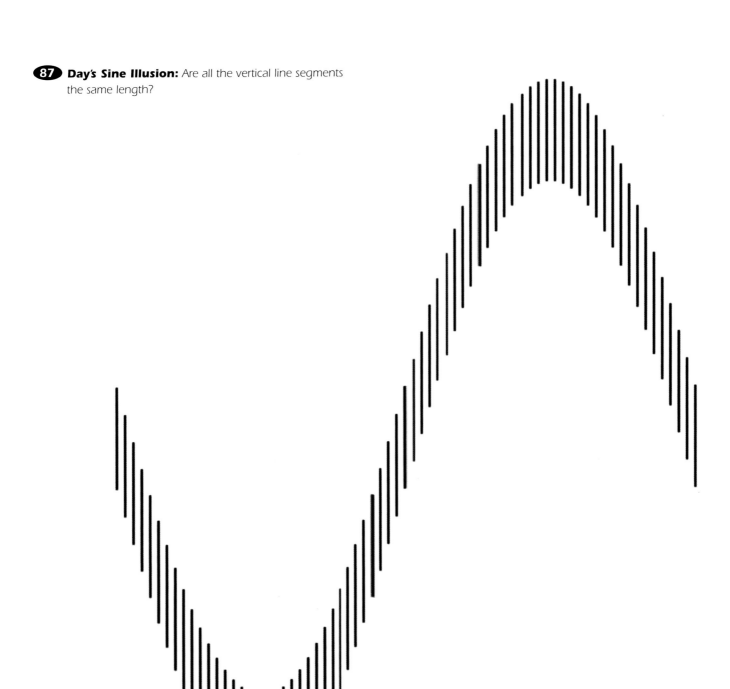

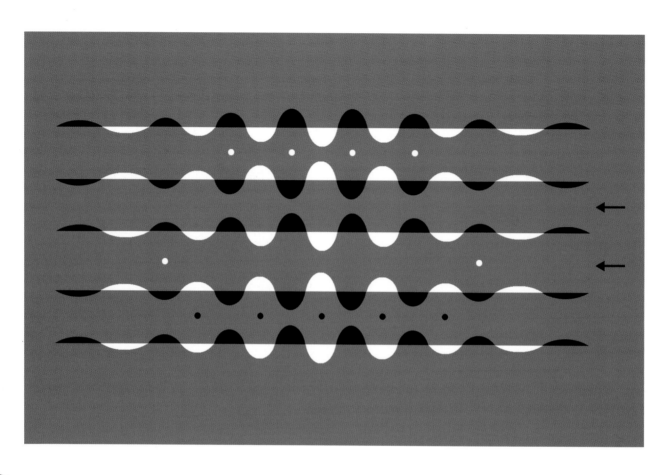

88 **Adelson's Mondrian Illusion:** The two arrows point to two bands of differing lightness. Does the top band appear darker than the bottom band?

89 **Chevreul Illusion:** Is the contrast of the adjacent rectangles the same throughout? Try covering the border between any two adjacent rectangles with a pencil. What happens?

90 **Soldier of the Lattice Fence:** This warrior is off to fight an impossible battle in this lovely drawing by Swiss artist Sandro Del Prete.

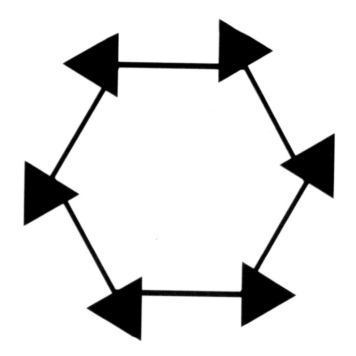

91 **Gerbino's Illusion:** Do the straight-line segments, if connected, appear to form a perfect hexagon?

92 **Hidden Profile of a Queen and her Husband:** Can you find the profiles of Queen Elizabeth II and her husband Prince Phillip?

93 **Perspective Arcade:** Why does this man look too large for the corridor?

94 **Bidwell's ghost:** You will need to perform this experiment in a completely darkened room. It is important that no light be leaking into the room. You will also need a flash camera and a color picture from a magazine.

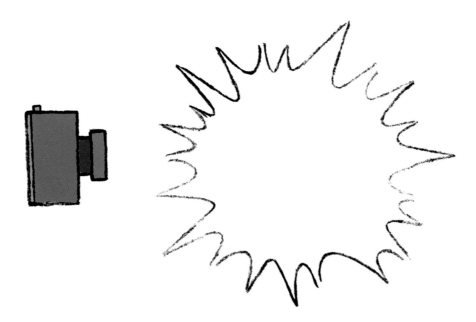

Completely adapt to the total darkness for several minutes (no less than seven – the longer that you adapt, the better the effect). Open the magazine up before you, look down in the direction of the magazine, and set the camera flash off (making sure that the flash is not pointed in the direction of your eyes, but in the direction of the magazine). Do not move your eyes. What happens?

Also, take a flash while holding your hand in front of your face. Then quickly move your hand behind your head. What you see and what you sense are in contradiction, which is a really eerie feeling.

95 **Reutersvärd's Fork:** What is wrong with this figure? Can you spot the problem quickly?

96 **Domino Face:** American artist Ken Knowlton created this portrait made entirely out of dominoes. The subject in the picture is Joseph Scala, a computer graphics artist and friend of Ken Knowlton. The piece is five feet tall. 'I shot a picture of Joe in his kitchen holding a domino,' Knowlton says. 'I put the photo through one computer program to digitize each tiny area into a shade of gray, then another to establish pairings of cells in the optimal way.' Knowlton used 24 complete sets of double-nine dominos. With 55 in each set, from blank-blank to nine-nine, the piece has 1,320 dominos in all.

97 Craik-O'Brien-Cornsweet Squares: Do the two gray squares appear to be identical or dissimilar in brightness?

98 **Nomad:** Note how the two figures transform into the face in this ambiguous illustration by Swiss artist Sandro Del Prete.

99 **The Ganzfeld Effect:** This is a very bizarre experience, which will cause you to have a feeling of blindness. Don't worry, it is completely harmless, and you can stop the effect at will.

You will need a ping pong ball, which is cut in half and a diffused light source, like a fluorescent lamp.

Place the two halves of the ping pong balls over each eye as in the picture. Gaze through them at the fluorescent light for at least five minutes. It is important that you only see diffused contourless light. Do not make any movements which will interfere with your gaze or cast shadows. After a while you will suddenly feel that you cannot see. This feeling of blindness is called 'blank out'.

If someone now casts a shadow over part of your visual field (say a pencil across the path of light), your vision will immediately return with the introduction of this contour!

100 An Impossibility within an Impossible Triangle: Swedish artist Oscar Reutersvärd gives us another variation of the impossible triangle.

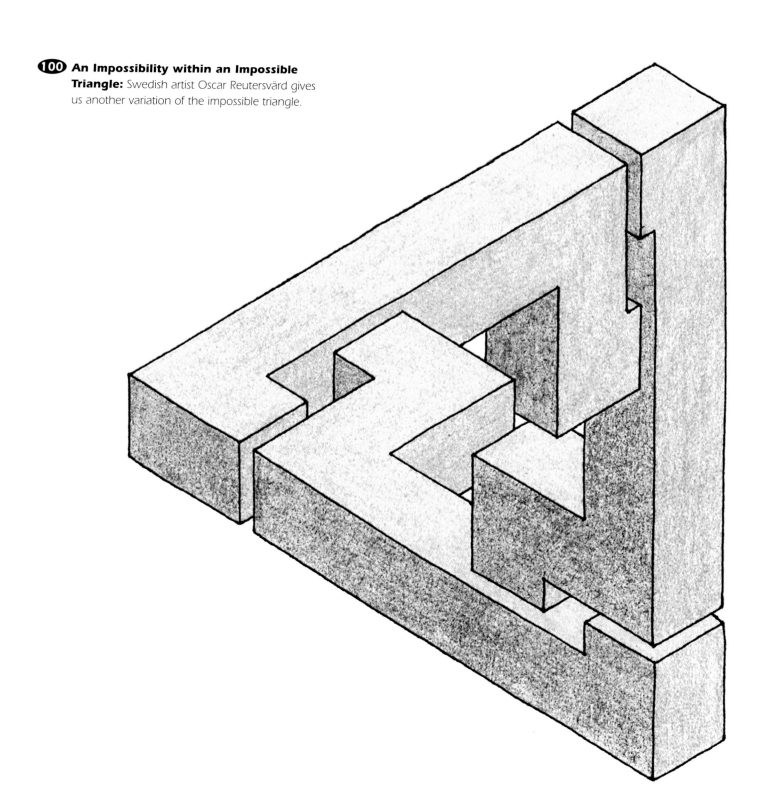

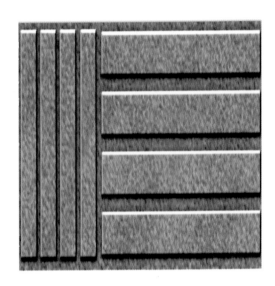

101 **In or Out:** Do the narrow vertical bands and the broad horizontal bands appear to be raised? Turn the image upside down and how do they appear now?

102 Van Gogh's Sunflowers:
You can see a reflection of Van Gogh's famous Sunflowers in the mirror hanging on the wall. This is a reflection of the distorted three-dimensional anamorphic sculpture lying horizontally before it. Japanese artist Shigeo Fukuda created this anamorphic sculpture.

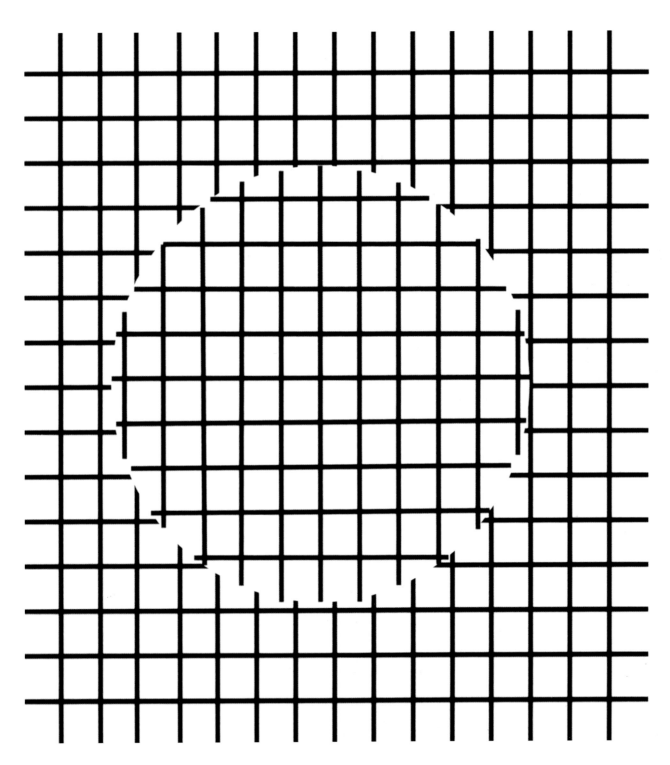

103 **Illusory Circle:** *Can you see the illusory circle even though there are no edges or contours to define it?*

Notes on Gallery III

72. Miniature Theater

In assessing size and distance relationships, your brain interprets the images projected onto the back of your retinas. When objects recede into the distance against a normal perspective background, not only does their visual angle get smaller, but they also approach a visual horizon. In the case of the Miniature Theater, the two waving girls are physically far in the distance, so their visual angle is small. The girls' relation to the true horizon is obscured, so that they look tiny when viewed through the aperture. This exhibit is in the famed Deutsches Museum in Germany.

73. Reutersvärd Triangle with a Twist

Look at the top portion of the two bars. One bar passes behind and merges with the other bar in an impossible way. A line normally cannot change its interpretation from convex (as when two surfaces meet away from the viewer) to concave (when two surfaces meet pointing toward the viewer), or vice versa, without passing through a vertex. The upper portion of the lighter colored surface ends in a Y vertex on its right side, with the middle segment being concave. As that segment extends upward toward the red cube it becomes convex without passing through a vertex, clearly an impossibility.

74. Bulging Lines

The lines are all straight. This is another example of a twisted cord illusion by Japanese artist and vision scientist Akiyoshi Kitaoka.

77. Hidden Illusion

It is the figure of a man's face wearing glasses. The lines forming the image are just slightly thicker than the continuation of the rest of the line. This illusion was created by Nicholas Wade.

78. Impossible Fold

This fold is perfectly possible with a rectangular piece of paper. It requires two cuts on either side of the long side of the rectangle about one third of the way down from each side. One side is folded under so that it is now on the opposite side, so you assume that it is the same side as the section of paper at the other end.

79. Neon Color Spreading

The illusory square on the left has a faint bluish color from a phenomenon know as neon-color spreading although the inside of the square is perfectly white. The vertices form the edges of a surface. The visual system tends to spread color within a bounded surface. On the right, when circles are placed at the edges of the illusory square, the neon color disappears. English vision scientist Marc Albert created this demonstration.

82. Perceived Gaze Illusion

There are at least two components to how we determine the direction of gaze. The first is the location of the eye in the eye socket and the second is the direction in which the head is pointed. We normally combine these two sources to determine the direction of gaze. In this case, we have an illusion, because mirroring the image on the right – except for the eyes, which remain unchanged (not reversed) – created the image on the left. This causes a dramatic change in the perceived direction of her gaze. Harvard vision scientist Shinki Ando created this Mona Lisa gaze illusion. W H Wollaston first noticed this effect in 1824.

83. Tiger Photomozaic

The tiger photomozaic was created on a computer with a specialized software program that evaluates the source image, in this case a tiger, in terms of relative values of light, dark, color, edges, and so forth. Once it assigns a numerical value to the source image, it then searches through a database of thousands of images (already stored on the computer) to find the best possible match. The computer will do a pretty good job, but an artist always needs to come in to make it look really good and touch up those areas which the computer missed.

84. Neon Color Spreading 2

The intersections of the black grid are replaced by blue crosses. It looks as if the blue spreads around the crosses and forms blue transparent disks in front of the crossings. A similar illusion without color spreading is also found in Ehrenstein figures. This illusion is associated with color assimilation as well as with illusory contours. In this case, illusory contours are seen based on the color change of the lines, and the color of the lines spreads over the region between the lines. Why does the color spread? This illusion may also be due to the filling in of a uniform surface with a particular color and brightness.

85. Mirror Symmetry of Faces

In the bottom photograph Hillary Clinton's face appears distorted, because her face has been digitally altered to be symmetrical. Most people's faces are slightly asymmetrical. However, it is not true, as maintained in the majority of perception books and articles, that because of this we subconsciously expect people's faces to look symmetrical. If a face is truly symmetrical, and done convincingly by a professional digital artist, a truly symmetrical face does not look strange at all – in fact, just the opposite. It is the sloppiness of the digital artist, as in this example, that gives rise to the perception that the face is distorted, not the fact that the face is symmetrical.

86. Blind Spot Illusion

The blind spot is an area of the retina where the nerves and blood cells of the eye pass through. Because there are no photoreceptors there, the brain fills in the gap with its best guess so that you don't notice that part of the world that you are looking at is missing.

87. Day's Sine Illusion

All the vertical segments are the same length throughout. It should be noted that the lines appear longest where the pattern is the thickest, but it remains speculation whether this has anything to do with creating the effect.

88. Adelson's Mondrian Illusion

The gray stripes are identical. MIT vision scientist Ted Adelson modified the standard simultaneous contrast illusion with the addition of transparent horizontal stripes, which augment the illusion.

89. Chevreul Illusion

When you place a pencil over the borders between any two adjacent rectangles, the two rectangles appear identical. in brightness. Yet, they are not identical. We are primarily sensitive to sharp differences in brightness, as exists at the borders between the rectangles. When these are covered, all that remains is a slight gradient, to which we are largely insensitive. This is known as Chevreul's Illusion.

91. Gerbino's Illusion

The lines, if connected, would form a perfect hexagon. The points where they would connect are 'masked' by the triangles. The visual system tends to continue lines when they disappear behind an occluding object, as they do in this case. The end point of each segment appears to be near the center of each triangle, which causes the perception of misalignment. Italian vision scientist Walter Gerbino created this illusion.

92. Hidden Profile of a Queen and her Husband

This vase is based on the famous two-dimensional figure ground illusion of Danish psychologist Edgar Rubin. This goblet, based on Rubin's concept, was made as a gift for the silver jubilee anniversary of Queen Elizabeth II and her husband, Prince Philip. If you view the dark area as the figure, instead of the ground, you will see the outlines of the two profiles (facing each other) on either side of the goblet. The Queen and her husband were delighted with the gift.

93. Borromini's Perspective Arcade

This illusion arcade, which can be found in the inner courtyard of Palazzo Spada, Rome, gives a false impression of depth. The columns literally get smaller the farther back they go, as do the ceiling coffers; the floor slopes upwards; and the cornices downwards; the columns are thicker at the front than the back; and the 'squares' on the pavement are actually trapezoids. Francesco Borromini, one of the most important architects of the 1600s, created it.

94. Bidwell's Ghost

After the glare of the flash wears off you should see a positive afterimage of the magazine and the room – a sort of exact snapshot. It is very important that you keep your eyes steady during this period otherwise you will lose the image. The positive afterimage may fade out after a few seconds, but will return as a negative afterimage, with each color replaced by its complementary color. This negative afterimage will be more persistent. There are many experiments that you can do with this set-up, involving changing the size of the afterimage by looking at distant objects, reading letters, and changing one's position after you have built up an afterimage. This phenomenon was first reported by the English physicist Shelford Bidwell in 1894 and thereafter became known as 'Bidwell's ghost'.

95. Reutersvärd's Fork

Some people do not understand conceptually why certain impossible figures, such as the impossible triangle, are impossible as real objects. There are other impossible figures that violate such basic ways that we interpret two-dimensional information into three-dimensional mental constructs that almost all people see the paradox immediately. This impossible figure by Swedish artist Oscar Reutersvärd is one such example, where figure and ground merge in an impossible way. This means that there is a qualitative difference between the type of paradox and how your visual system interprets this suggestion of a real three-dimensional object.

97. Craik-O'Brien-Cornsweet Squares

This variation on the simultaneous contrast illusion shows that a small border is enough to make the two identical gray squares look different in lightness. This is known as the Craik O'Brien Cornsweet illusion.

99. The Ganzfeld Effect

Contours are the basic building blocks of visual perception; in their absence we actually lose our ability to see. This Ganzfeld demonstration eliminates contours in your visual field, so vision fails. When a contour, or any luminance change, is perceived, vision immediately returns. A blank out can also occur in natural environments. Snow blindness is a kind of natural blank out, caused by the lack of contour in the retinal image when the visual field contains a lot of snow and ice. The snow and ice scatter much of the light in all directions, and together are very uniform in texture, which creates a natural Ganzfeld effect.

101. In or Out

This is a shape from shading illusion. Normally, light comes from above, and the shadows in the first alignment are consistent with this interpretation. When you turn the image upside down, the visual system is guided by the same constraints about the direction of light, so it now assumes that the bands are depressed rather than raised. However, both interpretations are somewhat ambiguous, and it is possible to see either orientation as either raised or depressed.

103. Illusory Circle

This is known as a subjective contour, because the contours of the circle are not physically present. The construction of these contours requires sophisticated non-local (neurons from a substantial area of the brain) processing in the brain.

104 **Dalí's Anamorphosis:**

Photo A

Spanish surrealist painter Salvador Dalí also created anamorphic images. Compare this image with the adjoining image to see what is revealed in the reflective cylinder.

Photo B

The picture above has been turned upside down and a reflecting cylinder added. Do you see the knight and his horse in the reflection?

GALLERY
IV

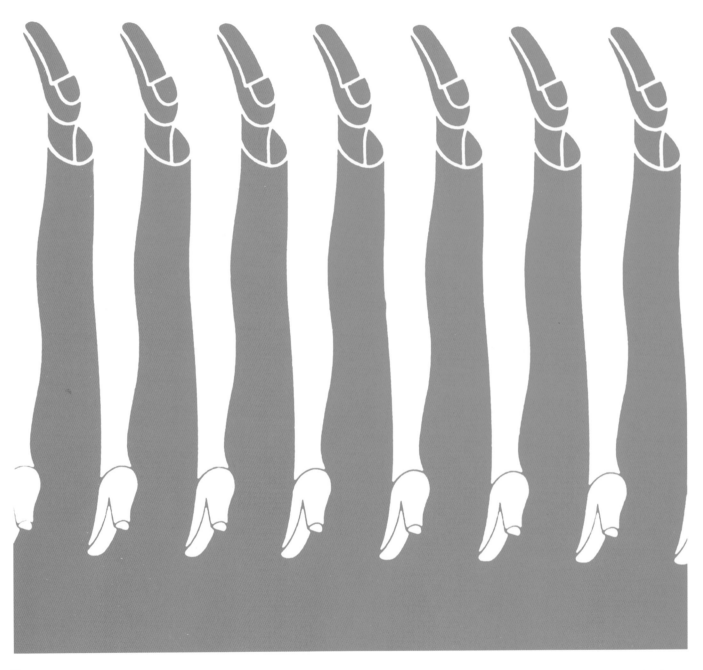

105 **Legs of two different Genders:** Are these men's legs or women's legs? This illustration is by Japanese artist Shigeo Fukuda.

Previous page: **Flip-Flop:** Are the red surfaces facing up or down? Keep looking: they will appear to flip to face the other direction due to contradictory depth cues. This ambiguous figure was provided by American artist Joan Miller.

106 Romeo and Juliet: In this drawing, Swiss artist Sandro Del Prete symbolically depicts the impossible barriers of love between Romeo and Juliet.

107 **Tessellating Escher:** This image contains multiple tessellating portraits of Dutch graphic artist M C Escher. Escher was famous for creating tessellating images. Turn the picture upside down and it still works. American artist Ken Landry created this tessellating topsy-turvy homage to Escher.

108 Belvedere: This is a physical model of an impossible building, based on the structure depicted in M C Escher's famous print, 'Belvedere'. The top floor is perpendicular to the bottom floor, yet they are perfectly joined. The ladder is also in a peculiar position. Japanese artist Shigeo Fukuda made this physical model.

109 **Beckoning Balusters:** Can you find the figures hiding in between the columns?

110 **Shape from Shading:** The top and bottom halves of this figure look like they are curving outward or inward, depending on whether you think the light comes from the left or right side. Try to imagine a light shining from the left – the top half will appear to curve out and the bottom half will appear to curve in. If you imagine the light as coming from the right side, then the top half looks like it curves inward.

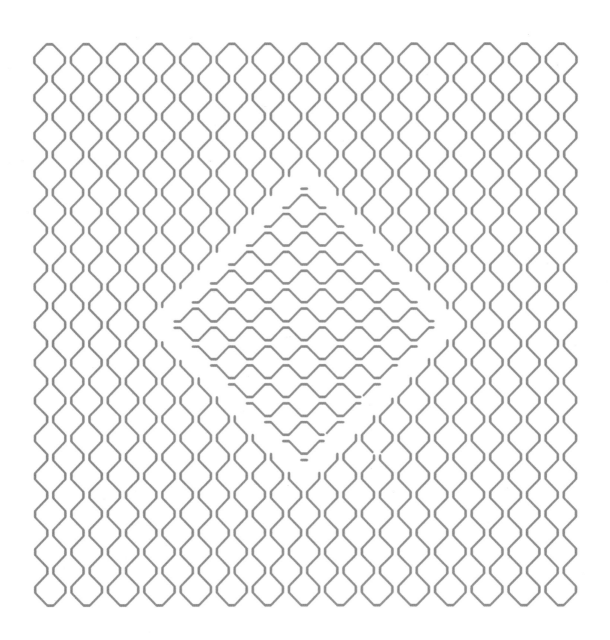

111 **A UFO Caught in a Mesh:** Move this illustration from side to side and you will see the center section move separately from the surrounding section.

112 **Afterimage:** Stare at this image for thirty seconds or more without averting your eyes or attention. Then quickly look at a blank sheet of paper. You will see a glowing afterimage.

113 More and More Human:
What's going on here?
Take a close look.

114 **Hidden Tools:** How many tools can you find?

115 **A Twist on Reginald Neal's 'Square of Three':** The three blue squares in the center appear to be tilted with respect to one another when placed against the background of Reginald Neal's famous painting 'Square of Three'.

116 **Nob's Impossible Ledge:** The plastic figure on the right is sitting on top of a wooden step, which corresponds to the piece separated on the right. If you follow the ledge to the left, you will see the other plastic figure sitting in a carved out depression, which corresponds to the separated piece on the left. How could this be possible?

117 **Assimilation Illusion:** Does the gray center square appear darker than the gray that surrounds it?

118 Can you spot the difference?: Are the five gray and white blocks all identical in color and brightness? Does a gray block appear to rest upon a lighter block in the prominent set of blocks in the foreground?

119 **Diamond Illusion:** Here are two rows of complete diamond shapes. Which row is darker – the bottom row or the top row?

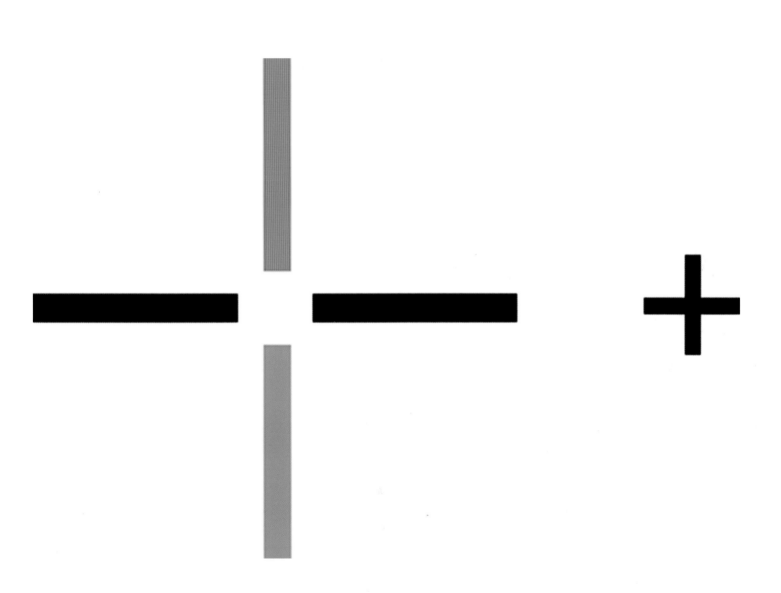

120 Color Blind Spot Illusion: In this blind spot illusion, close your right eye, and place the image so that the center blank square in the left figure falls in your blind spot. The formerly blank area will be filled-in. What color is the vertical arm over this area? Is it red? Is it green? Is it some other color? See illusion 86 for directions on how to locate your blind spot.

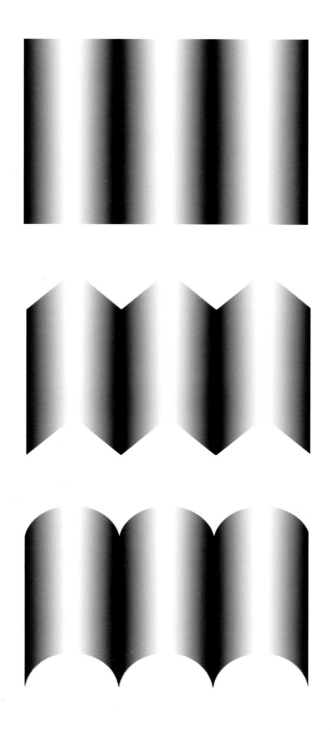

121 **Outline Can Determine Shape:** The figures depicted here appear to have three very different three-dimensional shapes, although their shading is identical. The only difference is the outline of the different shapes.

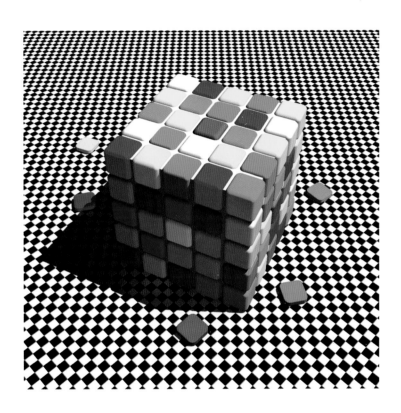

122 **Rubik's Cube Illusion:** Does the 'brown' square in the top of the Rubik's cube appear to be identical in color with the 'yellow' square that is in the middle of the side? They sure don't appear to be identical in color, yet haven't we fooled you so far?

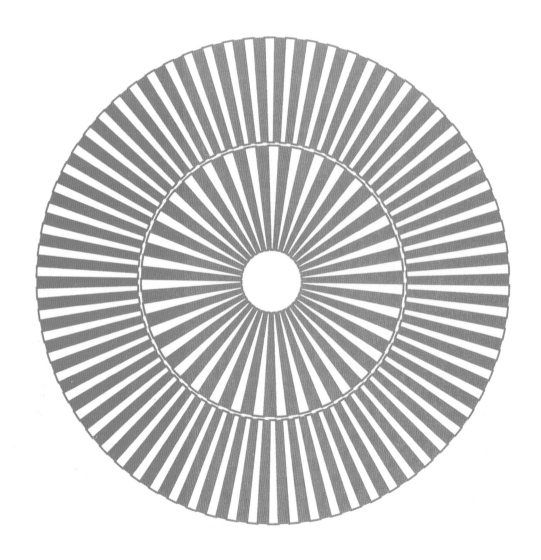

123 **The Hula-Hoop Illusion:** View this figure while giving the page a wide circular movement, but do not change the figure's orientation.

124 **Stone Windows:** A typical building in New York City, or is it? Perhaps if you compare the larger photo with the photo inset, you will notice that one side of the building is almost entirely painted. The artist is Richard Haas and he entitled this work '112 Prince Street Facade'. Note the painted side includes open windows, pulled shades, and air conditioners (with shadows). This form of artwork is known as trompe l'oeil.

125 **Impossible Staircase:** This is a
physical model of an impossible
staircase. Can you find either the
bottom or top stair? To see how
the model was made look at the
bottom photograph.

Photo A

Photo B

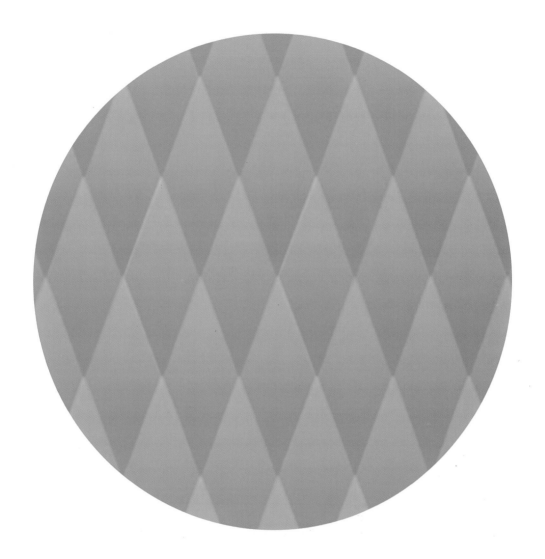

126 **Colored Diamonds:** *Are the diamonds all identical in their shade of green?*

127 Exploding Squares: Do the squares appear to be exploding?

128 **A King and His Queen:** This gruff, bearded king, drawn by artist Rex Whistler, is frowning because he can't seem to find his queen. He is ready to turn his whole kingdom upside down to find her. Do you think he will be successful? Can you find her?

129 **Anamorphic Stairs:** From one angle, the figure on the stairs appears perfectly normal, but when you see the same figure from a different angle, it appears quite distorted.

130 **Tilt Induction Effect:** Do the vertical bars appear to be tilted?

131 **Fisheye Illusion:** Using only one eye, bring the image within 3 cm of your eye. Do the curved lines now look straight?

132 **Bottom's Up:** Where is the bottom and top of the hole that the figures are sitting upon?

Jos
de mey
1993

133 **Still Life in an Impossible Windowsill:** Flemish artist Jos De Mey captured this still life in his windowsill. How can this be?

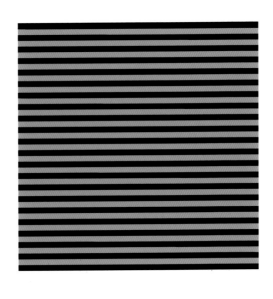

134 **Bezold Effect:** Compare the red horizontal lines in both figures. Do they appear to be an identical shade of red?

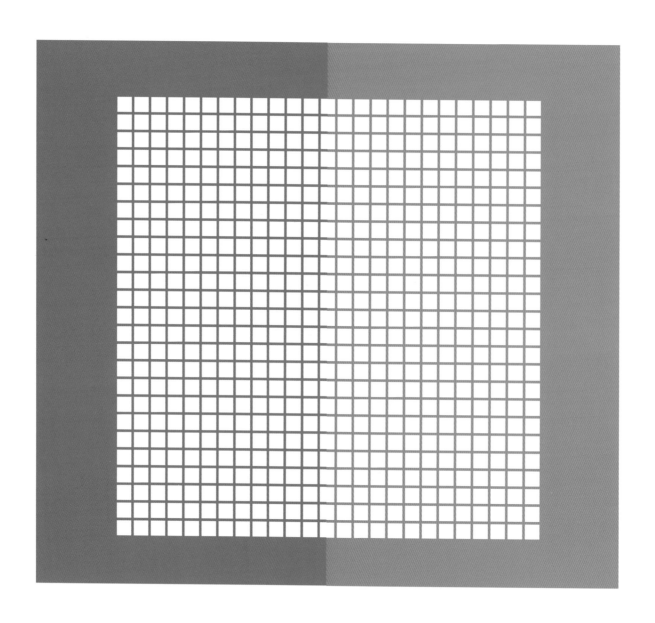

135 Color Assimilation: Do you perceive a reddish hue within the white squares on the right and a bluish hue within the white squares on the left?

136 Reflections of an Impossible Object: The reflection of this object in the mirror looks like an impossible rectangle, but its true form can be seen in front of the mirror.

Notes on Gallery IV

109. Beckoning Balusters
The standing figures are found in between the columns. The outlines of the opposing columns form their outline.

110. Shape from Shading
Your brain uses clues to determine depth from a two-dimensional picture. One clue is shading. In this illusion the shading is ambiguous. Thus, depending upon where your brain perceives the light is coming from, the shading will dictate whether the bulges are perceived as convex or concave.

111. A UFO Caught in a Mesh
Japanese vision scientist Akiyoshi Kitaoka created this variation of the Ouchi apparent motion illusion. The intersections between the vertical texture and the horizontal texture seem to trigger your visual system's motion detectors in different ways. When the page is moved back and forth you will perceive illusory motion in depth.

112. Afterimage
When you focus on the woman's face, light-sensitive photoreceptors (whose job it is to convert light into electrical activity) in your retina respond to the incoming light. Other neurons that receive input from these photoreceptors respond as well. As you continue to stare at the face your photoreceptors become desensitized. Your photopigment is 'bleached' by this constant stimulation. The desensitization is strongest for cells viewing the brightest part of the figure, but weaker for cells viewing the darkest part of the figure. When you quickly look at a white sheet, the least depleted cells respond more strongly than their neighbors, producing the brightest part of the afterimage: the glowing face. This is a negative afterimage, in which bright areas of the figure turn dark and vice versa. Positive afterimages also exist. Most afterimages last only a few seconds to a minute, since in the absence of strong stimulation, most nerve cells quickly readjust.

 Afterimages are constantly with us. When we view a bright flash of light, briefly look at the sun, or are blinded by the headlights of an approaching car at night, we see both positive and negative afterimages.

115. A Twist on Reginald Neal's 'Square of Three'
Radiating lines and other such geometrical background configurations can distort one's perception of lines and shapes. In this case, the three perfect squares appear to be distorted when placed against such a background. This illusion belongs to a class of illusions known as angle-expansion illusions. It is not perfectly understood what causes this illusion.

116. Nob's Impossible Ledge
This wooden model, created by Japanese puzzle inventor Nob Yoshigahara, is impossible only from this one viewpoint. This time we won't reveal the solution. We want you to think about it.

117. Assimilation Illusion
The gray in the middle box and the surrounding gray are identical. A gray background crossed by fine dark lines produces a darker gray. Conversely, the fine white lines will pull the value of the gray background toward the white. This is an assimilation illusion.

118. Can You Spot the Difference?
The blocks are not all identical in color, although they appear to be. The set of blocks in the far-left background and the prominent set of blocks in the foreground are identical with each other, but not identical with the remaining blocks. Cover the middle portion of the prominent middle set of blocks. You will see that although it appears to be a darker block resting on top of a lighter block, both blocks are identical. This is true also of the set of blocks in the far-left background. The other blocks, however, are made out of a gray

block and a lighter block. So in this image, there is a set of blocks that fools you, and a set of blocks that does not fool you, yet the dissimilar sets of blocks give rise to the very same perception! This scene combines perspective, orientation, texture, additional gradients and objects, and a distinctive background (the areas surrounding the two surfaces, i.e., the sky and ground, have the same average luminance), in such a way that suggests that the two equiluminant blocks (the object in the foreground) have a high probability of being differently reflective surfaces in light and shadow respectively. Thus, reality doesn't matter to the visual system, it insists that the blocks 'must' be two different shades, even though they are not. Duke neuroscientists Dale Purves and R. Beau Lotto created this wonderful enhanced demonstration of the Cornsweet illusion.

119. Diamond Illusion
The bottom row of diamonds is identical with the middle row of diamonds. This is a variation on the Craik O'Brien Cornsweet simultaneous contrast illusion where a small border is enough to make the two identical pink diamonds look different in lightness.

121. Outline Can Determine Shape
Vision scientists have repeatedly shown how shading can dramatically influence your perception of a figure's three-dimensional shape. In this case, Japanese vision scientist Isao Watanabe demonstrates how three figures can have identical shading, yet suggest three very different and distinct three-dimensional shapes. The only difference is their outlines.

122. Rubik's Cube Illusion
Unbelievable as it seems, the 'brown' square on the top of the Rubik's cube is identical in color with the 'yellow' square that is in the middle of the cube's side. You can test this by covering everything except those two squares, and then when compared, you will see that they are identical. Duke University neuroscientists Dale Purves and R Beau Lotto have used this new illusion to show dramatically that color perception is based on past experience. The block image illustrates how changing the empirical meaning of a scene – in this case removing the confounding shadows – not only changes the brightness that people perceive, but also the colors.

123. The Hula-Hoop Illusion
View this figure while giving the page a wide circular movement, but do not change the figure's orientation. You should see the two circles move at differently perceived rates. Vision scientist Nicholas Wade first described the 'Hula-Hoop' illusion.

126. Colored Diamonds
All the diamonds are identical in their shade of green. This illusion is similar to illusion number 119.

127. Exploding Squares
The 'illusion of the flying squares' is created by attaching black squares in a special configuration that makes a three-dimensional impression. Every figure consists of squares and every angle is a right angle. There are no curves. The illusion is an orientation illusion specific to corner edges. The specific placement of the little dark squares around the edges of the larger white square causes your perception of the white square's border to be contracted. Japanese vision scientist Akiyoshi Kitaoka created this illusion.

128. A King and His Queen
To find the Queen, turn the image upside down. Rex Whistler, an English muralist who died in 1944, left behind a wonderful set of upside down portraits. In 1946, a London publisher posthumously published 15 of these topsy-turvy portraits in an invertible book appropriately entitled, *OHO*.

129. Anamorphic Stairs
Hungarian artist Istvan Orosz created this anamorphic figure of a person climbing a set of stairs. In a normal painting of a figure, the image does not appear to distort as you walk past it. In this anamorphic image, the viewing point is absolutely critical, and the image distorts as you walk by.

130. Tilt Induction Effect
Although the vertical bars appear to be tilted outwards, they are not. This is known as a tilt induction effect, where the vertical line appears slanted in the direction opposite to the context lines. This illusion is thought to have some relationship to the classic Zöllner illusion. The tilt induction effect is greater when the context lines are near vertical than when they are near horizontal. In the tilt induction effect, visual cues (the oblique lines) cause errors in the perception of orientation, owing to mistakes in judging visual context.

131. Fisheye Illusion
The curvature of the back of your retina introduces a distortion in the way you perceive the lines. You rarely, if ever, notice this distortion, because you normally do not use only one eye, where the image covers most of the retina.

134. Bezold Effect
The red horizontal lines are identical in both figures. This is known as the Bezold effect, where context can influence your perception of a surrounding color. In the Bezold effect, colors will appear to expand beyond their borders and mix with neighboring colors. It is the reverse of the much more familiar effect of simultaneous contrast in which a color tends to induce its opposite in hue, value and intensity upon an adjacent color. Viewing distance and angle change the appearance of colors and the pictorial structures. Look at the image with your eyes squinted: this may enhance the effect. The colors in two identical pictures appear to be different when one of them is turned by 90° and compared to the other.

135. Color Assimilation
The white squares on the red background look reddish, and those on the blue background look bluish. Thus, the white squares take on their background's colors. Such a phenomenon is called color assimilation. This is the opposite of color contrast. The contrast and assimilation phenomena are also found for brightness and darkness. While the physiological mechanisms for brightness and color contrast phenomena are well understood, how and when the assimilation occurs are not.

136. Reflections of an Impossible Object
This physical model of an impossible rectangle only works from one special angle. Its true construction is revealed in the mirror. Even when presented with the correct construction of the rectangle (as seen in the mirror), you brain will not reject its seemingly impossible construction (seen outside the mirror). This illustrates that there is a split between your conception of something and your perception of something. Your conception is ok, but your perception is fooled. Bruno Ernst constructed this physical model.

137. Priming Illusion
If you have your friend say the word 'white' ten times fast and then immediately associate it with a cow, you 'prime' the person to associate the word white with cow. They then incorrectly say the word 'milk'. The correct answer, of course, is 'water'.

137 Priming Illusion: Have your friends say the word 'white' ten times fast. Then have them respond very quickly, without time for thought, to the following question, 'What does a cow drink?'

Glossary

Accommodation

Accommodation is the process by which the lens of the eye varies its focus when looking at objects of differing distances. Accommodation may serve as a weak depth cue over short distances.

Afterimage

An Afterimage is the visual persistence of a retinal image after the stimulus is gone. It is due to either intense or prolonged stimulation with constant eye fixation. Most people are used to the experience of afterimages after briefly staring at the sun or a bright light source, and seeing the resulting afterimage, which eventually fades out. Both positive and negative afterimages exist.

Ambiguous Figure

Ambiguous figures are single images which can give rise to two or more distinct perceptual interpretations. Most people find that one interpretation can switch to another readily, but they never can see both interpretations at once. It is common for the percepts to flip-flop, depending on various factors.

Anamorphic Image

Anamorphic images are drawings which have been stretched or distorted in a way so that their 'normal' configuration is revealed only on a reflected surface or from a particular critical viewing angle.

Attention

Attention is the concentration on a particular stimulus, sensation, or thought while excluding others. Attention is a broad term that probably covers more than one type of brain mechanism.

Blind spot

The blind spot is a region of the retina in which there are no receptors because the axons of ganglion cells exit the eye and pass into the optic nerve. Therefore this is an area without photoreceptors and hence this region shows no response to light.

Brightness

Brightness is the perceived intensity of light coming from the image itself, rather than any property of the portrayed scene. Brightness is sometimes defined as perceived luminance.

Cones

Cones are short, thick, tapering nerve cells in the photoreceptive layer of the retina which are specialized for bright-light and color vision. There are three types of cone-shaped photoreceptors that are responsible for the perception of color. Cones are heavily concentrated in the center of the retina (the fovea), but some are found throughout the periphery.

Contour

A contour is any place in the retinal image where the light intensity changes abruptly. It is the boundary of a region. Normally it is an edge that is assigned to the region of one side or the other, depending upon several factors influencing figure/ground organization.

Contrast

The contrast between two adjacent regions is their relative luminance levels.

Cues

Cues are features of visual stimuli which prompt the perception of depth or vision.

Filling-in

Filling-in is an action by the brain which 'guesses' the nature of absent information by assuming that it resembles related information.

Figure

Figure refers to an image region to which its contours have been assigned, producing the perception of being a perceptual element whose shape is defined by the contour and that 'stands out' in the center of attention.

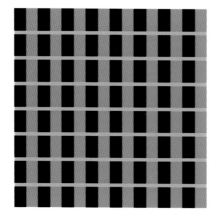

Global

Global refers to the overall arrangement of parts of a figure, as opposed to the local details or parts that make up the overall figure.

Ground

Ground refers to regions to which contours have not been assigned (see *Figure*), producing the perception of being in the background and extending behind the figure.

Illusory contours (or Subjective Contours)

Illusory contours are visual experiences of edges where no corresponding physical luminance edges are present in the image.

Impossible Figure

Impossible figures are two-dimensional line drawings which initially suggest the perception of a coherent three-dimensional object that is physically impossible to construct in a straightforward way.

Impossible Object

Impossible objects are physical objects, as opposed to two-dimensional drawings, that suggest an impossible construction. These objects usually require a specialized viewing angle to see the paradox.

Lateral inhibition

Lateral inhibition is the process of adjacent neurons inhibiting one another.

Lens Accommodation

See *Accommodation*.

Lightness

Lightness is the perceived reflectance of a surface. It represents the visual system's attempt to extract reflectance based on the luminances in the scene.

Luminance

Luminance is the amount of visible light which comes to the eye from a surface.

Optic Nerve

The optic nerve is the collection of axons from retinal ganglion cells as they exit the eye.

Perception

Perception is the conscious experience of objects and object relationships.

Orientation

Orientation is the property of objects concerning their alignment with respect to some reference line, such as gravity or the medial axis of the head.

Reflectance

Reflectance is the proportion of incident light that is reflected from a surface.

Retina

The retina is the curved surface at the back of the eye that is densely covered with over 100 million light-sensitive photoreceptors plus other sensory neurons (amacrine, bipolar, ganglion, and horizontal cells) which process the output of the receptors. Curiously enough, the photoreceptors are situated in the innermost layer while the ganglion cells, whose axons project to the brain, lie in the outermost layer, nearer to the lens of the eye. For this reason there has to be a gap in the retina through which the axons of ganglion cells can pass on their way to the brain. This gap in the photoreceptor layer produces a blind spot in each eye.

Retinal Image

The retinal image is the two-dimensional distribution of light of various intensities and wavelengths on the retina.

Rods

Rods are long, thin, cylindrical photoreceptors in the retina, used exclusively for vision at low levels of illumination. Rods are extremely sensitive to light and are located everywhere in the retina except at its very center (fovea).

Salient

An object is said to be **salient** if it attracts attention; stands out conspicuously

Sensation

Sensation is the simple conscious experience associated with a stimulus.

Shape Constancy

Shape constancy is the process by which the apparent shape of an object remains constant despite changes in the shape of the retinal image.

Size Constancy

Size constancy is the stability of perceived size despite changes in objective distance and retinal image size.

Tessellation

A tessellation is a tiling (or repeated design) which can be extended infinitely in any direction.

Vestibular System

The **vestibular system** monitors the body's movement and orientation in space and is the principle organ of balance and is located in the middle ear.

Visual Angle

Visual angle is a measure of image size on the retina, corresponding to the number of degrees the image subtends from its extremes to the focal point of the eye

Visual Field

The **visual field** is comprised of all the stimuli you can see, even those a few degrees away from the center of your focus.